Community Control of Economic Development

Rita Mae Kelly

The Praeger Special Studies program—
utilizing the most modern and efficient book
production techniques and a selective
worldwide distribution network—makes
available to the academic, government, and
business communities significant, timely
research in U.S. and international economic, social, and political development.

Community Control of Economic Development

The Boards of Directors of Community Development Corporations

PRAEGER SPECIAL STUDIES IN U.S. ECONOMIC, SOCIAL, AND POLITICAL ISSUES

Praeger Publishers   New York   London

Library of Congress Cataloging in Publication Data

Kelly, Rita Mae.
 Community control of economic development.

 (Praeger special studies in U.S. economic, social,
and political issues)
 Includes index.
 1. Community development corporations—United States.
2. Community leadership. 3. Directors of corporations—
United States. I. Title.
HN90.C6K43 1977   338.7'61'3092620973   77-7814
ISBN 0-03-022351-2

This book is a revised version of a study, "Community Participation
in Directing Economic Development," that was done by the author
under contract to the Center for Community Economic Development,
639 Massachusetts Avenue, Cambridge, Massachusetts 02139, and
published by them in 1976 as a federally funded grantee of the Community Services Administration.

PRAEGER SPECIAL STUDIES
200 Park Avenue, New York, N.Y., 10017, U.S.A.

Published in the United States of America in 1977
by Praeger Publishers,
A Division of Holt, Rinehart and Winston, CBS, Inc.

789 038 987654321

Printed in the United States of America

To
Patrick Joseph Kelly and Kathleen Theresa Kelly,
but for whom this book might never have been written.

ACKNOWLEDGMENTS

For encouraging me to undertake this project and for his continued support, I would like to thank Stewart E. Perry, the former director of the Center for Community Economic Development (CCED). His insightful comments and kind, but pointed, criticisms have helped me immeasurably. The Board Members Committee of the National Congress of Community Economic Development and its chairman, Arthur Choice of Nassau, New York, have also been of vital assistance. These individuals and the board members of the Community Development Corporations (CDC) who completed questionnaires for this study, along with the executive directors who cooperated, have made this study possible.

A special note of thanks must also go the Office of Economic Development staff of the Office of Economic Opportunity (OEO) for their cooperation in providing information on the CDCs and in completing a prepared questionnaire on the CDCs they monitored. I would like to thank Norman Gold, in particular, for the access to facilities and personnel that he helped provide. Abt Associates, Inc., and the Office of Economic Development both helped me obtain permission to use data collected during a three-year evaluation of the OEO-funded CDCs. Peter Merrill and Wendell Knox of Abt Associates personally assisted in preparing this data for use in this book.

I would also like to express appreciation to Rensis Likert for his permission to modify and adapt his Form S "Profile of Organizational Characteristics" for use in this study. His comments on my initial efforts to modify this profile were most helpful. I would like at the same time to absolve him of responsibility for any errors or inadequacies that remain in the final adaptation.

The editorial assistance of Leona Robbins of CCED and of Joyce Tovell has done much to improve the structure and readability of the final manuscript. I would also like to thank Vincent Peter Kelly and Stephen Michelson for their reviews of the manuscript and to acknowledge Martin Farber, Cheryl Gray, and Garmon West, Jr., for their assistance during the mail survey of the CDC board members. Garmon West completed most of the computer work required for this project.

I also wish to thank the following publishers for permission to cite and/or reproduce materials:

The Bobbs-Merrill Company, Inc., 4300 62nd Street, Indianapolis, Indiana 46268, for permission to reproduce a table from page 142 of *City Managers in Legislative Politics* by Ronald O. Loveridge, copyright © 1971, by the Bobbs-Merrill Company, Inc.

CONTENTS

LIST OF TABLES AND FIGURES

LIST OF ACRONYMS

BIA	Bureau of Indian Affairs
CDC	Community Development Corporations
CSA	Community Services Administration
ECCO	East Central Citizens Organization
EDA	Economic Development Administration
FBI	Federal Bureau of Investigation
FHA	Federal Housing Authority
FmHA	Farmers Home Administration
GMUDC	Greater Memphis Urban Development Corporation
HUD	U.S. Department of Housing and Urban Development
ICMA	International City Managers' Association
LITE	Lummi Indian Tribal Enterprises
LPPAC	Lawndale People's Planning and Action Conference
NLEDC	North Lawndale Economic Development Corporation
NOCDC	Northeastern Oklahoma Community Development Corporation
OEO	Office of Economic Opportunity
OMBE	U.S. Department of Commerce, Office of Minority Business Enterprise
PDC	People's Development Corporation
PIC	People's Involvement Corporation
SACDC	Southeast Alabama Community Development Corporation
SBA	Small Business Administration
SDN	Siete del Norte
SEASHA	South East Alabama Self-Help Association
SEEDCO	Seminole Employment and Economic Development Corporation
TELACU	The East Los Angeles Community Union
UICD	United Inner City Development Foundation
USEDC	Union Sarah Economic Development Corporation

Community Control of Economic Development

WHAT IS COMMUNITY ECONOMIC DEVELOPMENT?

The war on poverty of the 1960s and one of its offspring, the community control movement,[1] have left in their wake many unrealized and shattered programs. Only one major program area that bridges the war on poverty and the community control movement survives relatively intact. Community control of community economic development is still alive and thriving, with the support of federal funds, in at least 41 urban and rural U.S. communities.[2]

Because the process of community economic development itself is still unfolding and the individual personalities and communities involved in this ongoing "experiment" continue to exert their unique influences, the existing definitions are amorphous. Stewart E. Perry, who for many years was the director of the movement's main research support arm, the Center for Community Economic Development, describes it as follows:

> Community economic development is the creation or strengthening of economic organizations (or, more technically, economic institutions) that are controlled or owned by the residents of the area in which they are located or in which they will exert primary influence. The institutions that are owned or controlled locally can include such forms as business firms, industrial development parks, housing development corporations, banks, credit unions, and the cooperatives, and CDCs (community development corporations) themselves as the most broadly generalized, guiding institutions. They might also include organization (or services) that upgrade the human and social environment in such a way as to increase the economic value and energy of the community.[3]

By this definition, then, community economic development is something more than just economic development. It is the creating of new local businesses, identifying of new resources and talent, improving of the physical and social environment, and increasing of job and entrepreneurial opportunities. It is all the other things economic development consists of as well, but it is different in that the creating, identifying, improving, and so on are done under the guidance of the local residents. "The central and immediate goal of community economic development is to increase [the power and influence of the low-income community]. . . by providing economic muscle for a representative community organization."[4]

× The Community Development Corporation

The main vehicle for community economic development in the United States has been the community development corporation (CDC), an amalgamation of the leadership potential within the low-income neighborhood. CDCs have the responsibility of identifying not only the poverty problems of the community but also the means and resources available for launching an overall comprehensive community development effort. Their critical role has been likened to that of a machine tool, the core of industrial development, the lack of which has universally symbolized a backward, underdeveloped state. "The CDC, then, is a tool that turns out more tools. It turns out the ideas, the businesses, the services, and the organizations for influencing people outside the area in favor of the needs of the area."[5] The machine tool comparison is apt. The CDC must and does concern itself with the basic needs—human, financial, organizational, political, social, and economic—of all sectors of the community. By being a multipurpose community corporation, the CDC can not only plan development but also implement programs. If it does not have the means or the personnel to implement a policy, it can seek the skills of other organizations.

Although CDCs are not the only possible vehicles for implementing community economic development (in rural areas, for instance, cooperatives are common), they have predominated in the United States. This study concerns only those CDCs funded by the Office of Economic Opportunity.

Community Control of Community Economic Development

The community economic development movement as just defined was born during the turbulent 1960s.[6] The rioting in the ghettos had drawn attention to the poverty areas of the United States, particularly those that were black and urban. For the most part the government's response was to seek the reduction of tension by trying to ameliorate the physical environment and physiological conditions of the ghetto residents. The entire spectrum of public services, such as education for children and young adults (Head Start, job counseling, and manpower training programs) reflected concern for removing the psychological and sociological deficiencies of the ghettos and their residents. Little thought was given to developing ways of releasing already existing psychic energies.[7]

While most observers saw riot participation as evidence of social malignancy, some saw it as a sign that large numbers of blacks and other poor Americans had attained a new level of development, a level that compelled them to do for themselves whatever was to be done. In isolated parts of the country groups of these self-actualizing, growth-oriented leaders were seeking ways of making the environment into a set of opportunities for its inhabitants rather than a set of problems. In Cleveland, DeForest Brown led the effort to establish the Hough Area Development Corporation. Franklin Florence in Rochester, New York, brought FIGHT into being. In Philadelphia, the Reverend Leon Sullivan launched Zion Investment Associates. In each instance, black inner-city residents were seeking ways of beginning a comprehensive program of economic development. This program was to consist *of* them and to be run *by* them, and the benefits were most definitely to be *for* them.

A few influential whites also saw the need for wide-scale change. Senator Robert F. Kennedy, after a tour of Bedford-Stuyvesant, a black Brooklyn ghetto, concluded that the war on poverty needed a new approach. He realized that stressing the problems of individuals was not sufficient.[8] Primarily through his efforts and those of New York's other Senator, Jacob Javits, the Special Impact Program amendment, Title I-D of the Economic Opportunity Act of 1964, became effective in July 1966. This amendment signified a new approach; the poverty problem was now viewed as involving the total community, not just individual residents. For the first time, moreover, community business and economic development received equal emphasis with the service programs directed toward individuals.

The Office of Economic Opportunity (OEC) was the agency designated to implement this multipurpose, comprehensive development strategy. It foundered for several years, however, before actually developing an operating program. In 1967 it gave all of the money available to the Department of Labor, which used it primarily for more manpower programs. The only innovation immediately stemming from the legislation was the Bedford-Stuyvesant project, which was created by Senator Kennedy and his staff. Unlike those that had been started spontaneously in areas like Hough in Cleveland, Ohio, the Bedford-Stuyvesant project consisted first of a carefully selected group of influential business and financial figures in New York City, who were placed on the board of directors of the Development and Service Corporation. This lent enormous status and support to a separate board chosen by a leading black judge, who directed the all-black Bedford-Stuyvesant Restoration Corporation.[9] In 1974 the staffs of the two corporations merged administratively.

In spite of its creation by outsiders, the Bedford-Stuyvesant project was generally hailed by Congress. Interested congressmen began to apply pressure to

OEO to develop its entire program along these lines. Within OEO a group of planners sought to do this,* but in their opinion neighborhood community control had to be added in order to permit the residents themselves to define their problems and to set the objectives for development. These planners were especially convinced that to achieve the self-determination implicit in the community control concept it was essential to get young black males involved.[10]

Although the OEO staff recommended a strong, no-strings-attached program with 100 percent control by the community residents within designated poverty areas, the OEO director, Donald Rumsfeld, would not approve. Because of Rumsfeld's hesitation about this community control aspect, approval was given for an experimental program only. Early evaluation results in 1969 rated the OEO experiment successful in its efforts to initiate economic development in poverty areas,[11] but similar evaluations of the Department of Labor use of Special Impact Program funds indicated no such potential for change. In the next three years more CDCs were started, and in spite of hostility within OEO and other, largely administrative, problems, the CDCs performed reasonably well. In 1972 Congress passed a new amendment to the OEO legislation, Title VII, which authorized and funded Community Economic Development as a specific program, reviving it from the experimental category. It also legitimized the community control concept by specifically requiring that the funds be given to locally controlled community development corporations.[12] This legitimization of the concept, however, did not lead directly to full control by the residents. Even in 1977 control by the residents is not complete. While the overall strategies and objectives of the community development corporations are determined locally, final approval for specific investments must still be obtained from the federal funding agency. In 1974, however, a "venture autonomy system" was introduced that permits CDCs to make the final decisions on specific investment. Under this sytem the federal funding agency determines which CDCs are ready to finalize investments in local ventures with no federal supervision.

After the demise of OEO in 1975, the Community Services Administration (CSA) was charged with administering the program. Congress did not wish to discontinue or dilute the program by placing it within another existing agency. The heart of the program remains the community development corporation, the institution that is to plan and implement comprehensive community development programs. The guiding force of these corporations is the locally selected community-based board of directors.

As this brief history shows, the concepts of community economic development and community control have come a long way since 1967. Both now have

---

*The specific planners were an economist, James Robinson; a psychologist, T. M. Tomlinson; and two sociologists, Barbara Williams and Stewart E. Perry. Geoffrey Faux, from the Community Action Program, joined the planning group after the initial proposal was approved.

a firm foundation in legislation and in reality. Nonetheless, both the concepts and their main vehicles of implementation, the CDCs, remain in tender stages of growth. To enable them to have an "appreciable impact" on their communities, as the legislation requires, much still needs to be learned and done.

OBJECTIVES OF THIS STUDY

One of the most vital parts of the CDC program is the board of directors. As Perry states, "the key person in the entire process of community economic development is obviously the board member, selected by the community to guide the process. The question is, 'will he translate the ideas of community control and community development into reality?' "[13] Although the critical role of the CDC board of directors is generally recognized, very little is known about the boardmembers: who they are, how they define community economic development, and what they do as board members. The board members themselves generally are unsure about what others do and, on occasion, of what their duties and responsibilities are and/or ought to be. Although volumes have been written on the importance of maximum feasible participation of residents in low-income areas, very little is yet known about what difference, if any, such participation actually makes to the success or failure of an organization such as the CDC.

This lack of information on CDC board members and the ways in which they are in fact implementing the program design of community control of community economic development led the Center for Community Economic Development, which is the research support arm of CDC-funded CDCs, and the Board Members Committee of the National Congress of Community Economic Development, which is the national organization of community development corporations seeking to promote causes common to all CDCs, to sponsor this study. They wished to develop a nationwide data base on the leaders of community development corporations. The research itself was desired for the purposes of (1) developing information to release to the public in general and government officials in particular on the community economic development movement; (2) to providing CDC board members and executive directors with comparative and systematically analyzed information about each other's knowledge and experience; and (3) most essentially, obtaining information that would help board members define their jobs realistically, implement their responsibilities effectively, and relate productively to their CDCs and the communities they represent.

Several research topics are addressed. Chapter 2 presents a discussion of "The Nature of Community Entrepreneurship in Poverty Environments." Here the relationships between the somewhat socialistic-sounding community economic development movement and the American tradition of private enterprise and individual entrepreneurship are analyzed and the goals of the CDCs are described. Chapter 3, "Community Entrepreneurship and Control by Whom?" addresses the problem of who acutally exerts community control. Who in the low-income communities is selected to the CDC board of directors? What implications do the selection processes and the resulting compositions of the boards have for the democratically-based community control concept? Chapter 4, "The Process of Controlling the Community Development Corporation," examines the board members' definitions and performance of their various responsibilities. Special attention is paid to the relationahip of the board to its CDC and to analyzing the leadership interaction processes; the motivational processes; and the communication, decision-making, goal-setting, and other processes used to control the personnel and functions of the corporation.

Chapter 5, "Board Characteristics, Member Behavior, and the Success of the Community Development Corporation," raises the question of what difference do all of the above make for the success of the CDCs. Does it really matter that the board members differ in their backgrounds and behavior? If it matters, how does it matter? To what extent and in what ways are certain characteristics and behaviors, or the lack of them, related to the success of the CDC? In this chapter, also, specific assumptions about the need for and efficacy of community control are examined. Eleven basic hypotheses, ranging from the relationship of CDC success to the amount of participation in board activities, to the relationship of CDC success to accountability to the community, are tested. On the basis of the findings, conclusions are reached about the viability of the community control concept in the community economic development area and about the areas in which board members can most usefully spend their time.

Chapter 6, "Community Economic Development: Its Significance for Poor People and for Participatory Democracy and Community Control," attempts to tie the findings of the study together. It particularly addresses the basic issues of whether the CDCs are viable alternative forms for economic development in low-income areas; whether the CDCs are a new form of grass-roots and participatory democracy; whether the CDC governing boards actually have "community control"; and, finally, what effect citizen participation has on the success of the CDC.

RESEARCH METHODS

"Real" leadership and control of institutions are difficult to identify. Students of community power structures and decision making have often found that the officially designated and elected leaders are not always the people who make the basic decisions for the community.[14] Identifying the "real" leaders of the community development corporations would be a complicated task. Full agreement on such a group of persons probably would never be obtained. Our task here is not to examine all the possible leaders of the CDCs or even to determine the extent to which the official leadership of the CDCs actually control their organizations or community economic development in their areas. Our objective is limited to assessing who the official leaders of the CDCs are, what they have to say about the extent and effectiveness of their control, and what relationship exists, if any, between the characteristics and behavior of this official leadership and CDC success. The official leadership included consists of the board chairpersons, the board members, and the executive directors. Primary attention will be placed on the board members and chairpersons. (Although chairpersons are obviously also members of their boards the term "members" in this study includes only those members who are not chairpersons.)

Limitations of this Study

The data used in this study have been gathered only from CDCs funded by the OEO (CSA) and stem from two sources. One source is information that was collected, primarily in 1972, as part of an independent evaluation by Abt Associates, Inc., of the OEO-funded community development corporations.[15] During that evaluation a survey of CDC board members was completed as part of a larger survey that included board members of CDC subsidiaries. Of those interviewed, 340 board members were identified. They represented 28, or 76 percent, of the 37 CDCs funded in continental United States at that time and approximately 65 percent of all CDC board members.[16] The respondents had been randomly selected from a complete list of the board members. The interviews were completed at each CDC site by locally recruited interviewers. All CDCs and related personnel were required by OEO to participate in this evaluation survey. Those that were not included were excluded at the discretion of OEO and/or the evaluator. Exclusion was usually on the grounds that the CDC had either just started or was in the process of being terminated; but two CDCs, in Alaska and Hawaii, were excluded due to logistical difficulties and the costs of doing on-site research. Data from the Abt evaluation are also available on 24, or 65 percent, of the board chairpersons and 28 or 76 percent of the executive directors. These data, however, represent interviews from two different periods. In order to obtain a sufficient number of respondents to conduct statistical analyses, the data furnished by the chairpersons and directors interviewed in 1972 and those interviewed in early 1973 were combined, using the questions the two surveys had in common.

The second source of data (hereafter called the Kelly survey) is a mail survey of all known board members and chairpersons, which I conducted in the fall of 1973, directly for the purposes of this study. This survey was completely voluntary, with no directive from anyone that the CDCs must participate. By 1973 the readily available lists of board members held by the OEO, Abt Associates, and the CCED were no longer correct; hence for the Kelly survey a complete accurate listing had to be obtained from the CDCs as the survey proceeded. The Kelly questionnaire was first sent to board members in early August of 1973. In late August a follow-up letter was mailed. By mid-September 1973, 172 usable questionnaires had been returned. At this point about 53 percent of the rural and 33 percent of the urban board members had responded. Because of the greater response from rural areas, a relatively higher proportion of white board members had responded than nonwhite board members. In addition, few responses had been returned by board members of CDCs that had received $2 million or more from OEO since the CDCs' inception. In an effort to reduce these biases, a revised shortened questionnaire was prepared and mailed to all nonrespondents and a follow-up telephone call to each was made. An additional 101 usable questionnaires resulted.

The final Kelly sample of 273 seems to be representative of the 1973 CDC board members. Of the 35 CDCs then being funded in the continental United States, board members from 26, or 74 percent had responded. Four CDCs explicitly chose not to participate; two of these were in the middle of elections, and hence neither the members leaving nor the new ones entering desired to respond. Five other CDCs did not explicitly decline to participate, but fewer than one-third of the members of each responded, and hence they were excluded. From the 26 CDCs represented in the sample, 273, or 63 percent of the total number of 434 known board members completed the questionnaire. The rural-urban distribution was as follows: 72 percent of the possible 149 board members of the 11 participating rural CDCs responded, while 58 percent of the possible 285 board members of the 14 participating urban CDCs responded. In terms of the total amount of OEO funds the CDCs had received, the response rates were: 53 percent for the CDCs receiving $2 million or more (80 of a possible 150) and 68 percent for the CDCs receiving less than $2 million (194 of a possible 284).

A statistical analysis of the differences in response between the 172 persons who completed the long questionnaire and the 101 who completed the short questionnaire showed no significant differences on the variables of age, level of educational attainment, or length of time as a board member. Differences, however, were found on the variables of race, rural-urban location, and amount of funds the CDCs had received from OEO, as already noted. These statistical differences stem from the fact that the second wave of 101 questionnaires came heavily from nonwhite, urban board members, with a strong representation from the better-funded CDCs; the differences indicate that the original biases found in the first 172 responses were largely corrected by the additional 101 responses in the final sample of 273. Support for this conclusion is also derived from the percentage of whites in the final Kelly 1973 sample. This percentage—27 percent of 273—is almost identical with the percentage of whites in the Abt 1972 sample—28 percent of 340. In addition, an examination of the educational levels of the respondents and nonrespondents in five CDCs for which such information was available revealed no sharp differences. The more educated were just as likely to be nonrespondents as the less educated. Of the 26 participating CDCs, 19, or 73 percent, of the chairpersons responded, as did 20,

TABLE 1.1

Community Development Corporations Funded by the Office of Economic Opportunity that Are Included in the Study, by Rural-Urban Location

Urban CDCs (N = 19)	Rural CDCs (N = 16)
Black Economic Union (BEU), Kansas City, Mo.	Adela Development Corp., Utah Community Investment and
The Circle, Boston, Mass.	Development, Inc. (CIDI), Ark.
Community Action Organization, (CAO), Erie County, N.Y.	Delta Foundation, Miss. East Central Committee for
Denver CDC, Denver, Colo.	Opportunity (ECCO), Ga.
East Boston CDC, Boston, Mass.	Impact Seven, Inc., Wisconsin
East Central Citizens Organization (ECCO), Columbus, Ohio	Job Start, Ky. Lummi Indian Tribal Enter-
The East Los Angeles Community Union (TELACU). Los Angeles, Calif.	prises (LITE), Wash. Midwest Minnesota CDC, Minn.
Greater Memphis Urban Development Corp. (GMUDC), Memphis, Tenn.	Northeastern Oklahoma Community Development Corp.
Harlem Commonwealth Council, New York, N.Y.	(NOCDC), Okla. Seminole Employment and
Human Development Corp. (HDC), St. Louis, Mo.	Economic Development Corp. (SEEDCO), Fla.
Hough Area Development Corp., Cleveland, Ohio	Siete Del Norte (SDN), N.M. Southeast Alabama CDC, Ala.
Hunts Point Community Local Development Corporation (CLDC), South Bronx, New York, N.Y.	Southwest Virginia Community Development Fund, Va. Standing Rock Industries, N.D.
Inner-City Business Improvement Forum, Detroit, Mich.	TENCO Development, Tenn. Westside Planning Group, Fresno,
People's Involvement Corp./People's Development Corp. (PIC/PDC), Washington, D.C.	Calif.
Nassau County Community Economic Development Corporation (CEDC), Nassau County, N.Y.	
North Lawndale Economic Development Corp., Chicago, Ill.	
Southside Revitalization Corp. (SRC), Racine, Wisc.	
United Durham, Inc., Durham, N.C.	
United Inner City Development Foundation (UICDF), Seattle, Wash.	

Note: Due to logistic difficulties CEDC, Alaska, and Lokahi-Pacific CDC, Hawaii, were excluded from this study. Prior to 1972-73 three other CDCs—New Communities in Georgia, Las Colonias in Texas, and FIGHT in Rochester, N.Y.—also had received OEO funds, but they were terminated prior to either survey. The New Jersey Department of Community Affairs was excluded because it acts as a lending agency rather than a CDC. The board members of the Bedford-Stuyvesant Restoration Corporation did not participate in either survey.

Source: The basic data in this table on the geographical location of the CDCs are taken from Brian J. Reilly, "Distribution of SIP funds," *CCED Newsletter*, February 1973.

or 77 percent, of the 26 executive directors. Table 1.1 lists the CDCs included in the study by their rural-urban locations.

The reader is specifically asked to remember the biases noted in the sample of 172 when reading the data pertaining to the review and control functions of the boards. When it was found necessary to condense the original questionnaire, some of the items pertaining to these functions were deleted. At the time the choice had to be made, several items of the questionnaire in Section D, "Profile of the Board and the CDC" (see Appendix), were deemed sufficient, but in retrospect this judgment has proved to be erroneous. The results of the items asked of the 172 respondents are included only in those instances in which they provide potentially significant insights for our understanding of community control of economic development.

It should also be noted that different sample frames for the CDCs themselves were used in the Abt and Kelly surveys. Abt chose to concentrate on the 30 oldest CDCs funded by OEO, while I sought to include all 35 of the CDCs still being funded in 1973. The CDCs excluded by Abt, but included in the Kelly survey, tended to have a higher proportion of Spanish-speaking people than the 30 oldest CDCs. They also tended to have received less than $2 million to date from OEO. In addition, over three-fourths of the 9 CDCs that chose not to participate in the Kelly survey had been included in the Abt survey. Hence, although both final samples appear to be generally representative of the board members included within each sample frame, the differences in the sample frames make it difficult to reach reliable conclusions about changes over time on such matters as board member characteristics or board member behavior. For this reason discussions of changes over time are kept to a minimum.

Design of the Study

The basic concerns of this study involve issues of political participation and the effects such participation or its lack will have on a specific community-based organization, the community development corporation. The three chapters that present the empirical data of the Kelly and Abt surveys examine who the board members of the community development corporation are, what they do as board members, and how those functions affect the success of their organizations. Much of this information will be presented in tables in which two standard tests of statistical significance have been used. The chi square significance at the 95 percent level of confidence is indicated in the footnotes to the tables, as is a significant finding on the Fisher Exact one-tailed test at the 87 percent level of confidence or above. The exact probability for the Fisher Exact test is presented in those instances where the level of confidence is higher than 87 percent. In Chapter 5 the Kendall Tau C correlation, a measure of association of rank orders, will be noted as a column in the table or at the bottom of tables, whichever is most appropriate. Other standard terms and their abbreviations used are the number of respondents (N), probability (p), degrees of freedom (f) and the mathematical symbols for greater than ($>$) and less than ($<$). Thus in Table 4.2 footnote a means that the probability of the distribution differences noted in the percent of meetings attended by the urban and rural chairpersons occurring by chance was found to be less than 13 out of 100, using the Fisher Exact one-tailed statistical test. Footnote b in the same table means that the distribution differences in these columns would occur by chance less than 5 times out of 100. In other words, in neither case are the differences in attendance noted likely to be the result of chance factors. The absence of either footnote under "Total OEO Funding" in the same table means that these distributions could occur by chance.

Community control of organizations representing neighborhoods or other subpolitical entities is a matter of great concern to citizens and students of U.S. governmental processes. In Chapters 3 and 4 the basic purpose of the presentations is a description of who the board members are and what they are doing as CDC board members. In these chapters the findings from this study are compared, where possible and appropriate, with those of studies of other community-controlled institutions, with similar types and levels of participation and behavior by the political electorate at large, and with stated expectations of what such participation ought to be by experts on "maximum feasible participation." It is hoped that the analyses of empirical data from the survey and these comparisons with other data and statements on such participation will provide new and useful insights on the meaning and process of community control as well as simply describe the current status of CDC boards of directors.

Chapters 3 and 4, in addition to presenting the descriptive totals for all the CDCs studied, consistently examine the following two basic questions: Do the responses of the board members and chairpersons vary significantly depending upon the rural-urban location of the CDC? and Do they differ significantly depending upon the amount of money OEO has given the CDC since its inception? Differences in political participation and economic development between rural-urban areas and large and small organizations suggest that these subanalyses need to be performed.

Chapter 5 systematically examines some of the basic assumptions underlying the theory and practice of community control. The CDCs are placed on a 20-point success scale on the basis of judgments made in the fall of 1973 especially for this study by selected experts on CDCs—the OEO analysts responsible for the CDCs. (Details about the use of this questionnaire are in Chapter 5; the questionnaire is reproduced in the Appendix.) For most of the analyses the CDCs are placed into three groups: the least successful CDCs, the somewhat successful CDCs, and the most successful CDCs.

Using these success rankings as the dependent variable and the data presented in Chapters 3 and 4 as the independent variables, the following 11 hypotheses are examined. The success ranking of the CDC will be higher (1) the greater the participation of the board members in board activities; (2) the greater the involvement of the board of directors with CDC staff and activities; (3) the greater the interaction of the CDC leadership (board members, staff, and director); (4) the more the board members are motivated by community and CDC needs and not personal needs and status; (5) the more everyone on the board feels responsibility for achieving CDC goals; (6) the better the communication processes between the CDC staff and CDC board; (7) the greater the involvement of the board of directors in decision making in general; (8) when the most important decisions of a year concern the setting of specific goals and policies for operation, rather than when the board is concerned either with the broader long-term strategy or structural-functional problems of implementation and operation; (9) when board members participate in policy-related review and control functions rather than mediating between the CDC and other organizations, acting as CDC representatives, or actually engaging in the implementation of CDC policies; (10) the greater the board involvement in the review and control functions; and (11) the greater the board members' accountability to the target area community.

NOTES

1. The most well-known view (as well as one of the least favorable) of the community control concept is Daniel P. Moynihan, *Maximum Feasible Misunderstanding: Community Action in the War on Poverty* (New York: Free Press, 1969). For a contrasting view see Lillian Rubin, "Maximum Feasible Participation, The Origins, Implications, and Present Status," *Poverty and Human Resources Abstracts* (November-December 1967). For a presentation asserting that community control was never tried in the community action programs, see Stephen Rose, *The Betrayal of the Poor* (Cambridge, Mass.: Schenkman, 1972). Several case studies of community corporations and neighborhood boards are available in Howard W. Hallman, *Neighborhood Control of Public Programs: Case Studies of Community Corporations and Neighborhood Boards* (New York: Praeger, 1970).

2. Information on CDCs funded by the Office of Economic Opportunity and its derivative, the Community Services Administration, is available from the Center for Community Economic Development, 1878 Massachusetts Avenue, Cambridge, Mass. The CCED librarian, who will also make information available on CDCs not funded by OEO, should be consulted. Geoffrey Faux, *CDCs: New Hope for the Inner City* (New York: Twentieth Century Fund, 1971), also describes some of these non-OEO corporations.

3. Stewart E. Perry, *Federal Support for CDCs: Some of the History and Issues of Community Control* (Cambridge, Mass.: Center for Community Economic Development, 1973), p. 16.

4. Ibid., p. 17.

5. Ibid., p. 21.

6. Ibid.; Perry provides the most readable brief history of this movement available at present.

7. See Jeanne N. Knutson, *The Human Basis of the Polity: A Psychological Study of Political Men* (Chicago: Aldine-Atherton, 1972), for a comprehensive analysis of the relationship between the psychological needs of human beings and political and social activity. One point that she makes that is of particular interest to this discussion is that the provision of opportunities for growth is the only effective means of removing certain psychological needs. Simply meeting deficiencies at certain points of development is no longer sufficient.

8. See Jack Newfield, *Robert Kennedy: A Memoir* (New York: Bantam, 1970).

9. *Rebuilding Bedford-Stuyvesant: Community Economic Development in the Ghetto*, a case-study history of the Bedford-Stuyvesant CDC, its origins, activities, and development, has been prepared by Barry Stein of the Center for Community Economic Development (Cambridge, Mass.: CCED, 1975).

10. Perry, *Federal Support*, pp. 5-6.

11. See the Westinghouse Learning Corporation reports to OEO, January 1969 and July 1970; they are on file at the CCED library.

12. See Title VII of the Economic Opportunity Amendments of 1972 (Public Law 92-424, September 19, 1972).

13. Perry, *Federal Support*, p. 27.

14. Willis D. Hawley and James H. Svara provide an annotated bibliography of much of this literature in *The Study of Community Power: A Bibliographic Review* (Santa Barbara, Calif.; ABC-CLIO, 1972).

15. This three-year, large-scale evaluation resulted in several reports to OEO. These have been published under the general title, *An Evaluation of the Special Impact Program* (Cambridge, Mass.: Abt Associates). There is a Phase 1 Report, 4 vols., 1972; an Interim Report, 4 vols., 1973; and a Final Report, 4 vols., 1974. Those interested in the details of the sample design, sample frames, and interviewing procedures should see the appendix to Volume 4 of Phase I Report.

16. Personal communication from Peter Merrill of Abt Associates, July 1973.

2

THE NATURE OF COMMUNITY ENTREPRENEURSHIP IN POVERTY ENVIRONMENTS

THE IMPORTANCE OF ENTREPRENEURSHIP

In the United States it is a popular article of faith that continued U.S. growth and development depends upon entrepreneurs. Although the word "entrepreneurs" has come to include persons owning and operating their own businesses, their importance to the economy stems not so much from the performance of this managerial function as from their innovative abilities. While others plod along in the same old fashion, the entrepreneur devises new ways of combining the factors of production, that is, land, labor, and capital. The entrepreneur is the one who introduces the new products and the new processes of production, thereby increasing his or her own economic return and simultaneously benefiting all of society. While the businessman and the manager operate within established frameworks and policies, the entrepreneur seeks the unknown, investigating areas others either have never thought of or, because of past failure, no longer dare to approach.[1]

The stress upon the entrepreneur fits well into the American ideology and history of both capitalism and individualism. When we Americans think of past problems and crises, we think of them as problems and crises of individuals. When we think of solutions, we also tend to focus on individuals.

Hosts of twentieth-century scholars have documented this preoccupation with the individual. Artists have stressed the isolation and inequality of individuals before God, the economy, and the state. Social scientists have stressed anomie and alienation. The powerlessness, meaninglessness, normlessness, value isolation, self-estrangement, and even self-hatred of humankind have been the preoccupations of some of the best minds of this century.[2] Given this intellectual environment and U.S. history, in the 1960s it was natural to define the problems of urban ghettos and of poor Americans as problems of specific individuals. People were poor because they lacked specific characteristics, talents, or abilities, and this prevented them from getting jobs, services, and other private and public goods. The community did not have business institutions because of the absence of individual entrepreneurs. The deviancy of individuals from either accepted or ideal social norms was the essential problem. The solution, according to this view, was to eliminate the deficiencies and correct the deviations of the individuals involved.

Developing Individual Entrepreneurs

Unfortunately for a great many American poor people and also for the federal government, which spent millions of dollars on this individualistic approach, the problems of community deterioration are not affected on any meaningful level by such a solution. Low-income individuals throughout the world, and particularly in urban black ghettos, have not tended to organize economically. Their struggles have been highly individualistic. Their failures, however, have caused whole communities to disintegrate. The history of humankind reveals a parallel between the development of civilization and the development of organized cooperation and mutual aid. One pair of researchers, Burt Griffin and Zachary Paris, point out in a manuscript in process that until the late 1960s most U.S. low-income neighborhoods have been virtually "uncivilized" in this respect. What the individualistic focus has overlooked is the fact that organized mutual cooperation has been essential to the economic advancement and the entrepreneurial development, not only of all immigrant groups in the United States, but also of all underdeveloped nations. Disbursement of capital to a few individuals has not produced economic growth in poverty-ridden communities.

The utilitarian assumptions made by Adam Smith, Joseph Schumpeter, and other classical economists about the rationality of human behavior led these economists to believe that individuals will innovate in order to maximize the pleasures of profit and increased leisure and to minimize the pain of work. Nevertheless, can individuals innovate, can entrepreneurship flourish, without the support of certain social institutions and a beneficent environment? Max Weber believed that it was the rise of Protestantism, particularly Calvinism, and the Protestant ethic that had produced the needed ideology and attitudinal framework required for capitalism to develop. According to Weber, it was this change in thought and social institutions that gave rise to entrepreneurship and much of the Western World's economy as we know it today.[3] But what about the non-Protestants—the Irish, Italian, and Jewish immigrants? Did they not have entrepreneurs and economic development? The answer to this question is obviously yes; but again, one has to ask why.

According to Elliott D. Sclar, it was the extended family structure of the immigrant communities and their strong religious ties that united the community and made economic development possible.[4] Both permitted economies of scale that led to capital formation, and both fostered the development of community-oriented entrepreneurs. Sclar cites data gathered by Richard Sennett in a middle-class section of Chicago during the late nineteenth century that appear to offer support for his thesis. Sennett had written as follows:

> Sons of extended families were far more likely to become proprietors of businesses than those of nuclear families.[5]

Sclar concludes as follows:

> The issue of who becomes the entrepreneur and how he behaves, as important as it is, is certainly matched in importance, if not surpassed, by the issue of why he is encouraged to behave as he does. This is a function of the institutions which form the individual's values and perspectives. This was especially true in the case of the earlier immigrant groups. Whether the individual sought consciously or not to aid the community is not as important as the fact that the community and its values helped to create and channel entrepreneurial development to the needs of the entire community. In addition the institutions of the community were such that the income from such things as low skill work could be turned into capital for further development of the community. In effect, then, the experience of the immigrant communities made clear the need to reverse a rather popular causal sequence. Rather than the entrepreneur being an individual who pulls his community up the social ladder, he is a vehicle which the community uses to transport itself.[6]

Ivan H. Light, in his study *Ethnic Enterprise in America: Business and Welfare Among Chinese, Japanese, and Blacks*, also concludes that individual entrepreneurship has not been the source of economic success among these ethnic groups. He says:

> Hence, among both Chinese and Japanese, high rates of business proprietorship and low rates of welfare dependency were related in that both rates reflected the activities of mutually supportive, ascriptively bounded moral communities. Entrepreneurial individualism was not the cause.[7]

Light stresses that a major reason why blacks have not been as successful in business as the Chinese and Japanese is that individualism became rampant in the city slums, disorganizing black social life.

The comprehensive study by David C. McClelland, *The Achieving Society*, provides further support for the contention that individuals will not develop and function as effective entrepreneurs without a proper psychological environment and properly supporting social institutions.[8] In summarizing over 600 studies from more than 30 countries, McClelland reached, among others, the following conclusions:

1. Individuals with high achievement motivation are less likely to be motivated to action by monetary rewards than individuals low on achievement motivation.

2. High achievers score very high in "other-directedness" and are greatly influenced by public opinion. They are not independent of their communities, but rather accept what the community defines as success and push to achieve that success. Financial status is an index achievers use to indicate how well they are doing, not a criterion for what they ought to do.

3. "Group myths," affective warmth, and collective enthusiasm are important elements of the high achievers' outlook.

4. High achievers do not take extraordinary, heroic risks, but rather risks that are moderate and calculated, permitting them to have reasonable control over the outcome.

5. The high-achieving individual is not necessarily more self-disciplined or willing to work hard and long upon unpleasant and routine tasks in order to succeed. To the contrary, he or she tends to dislike routine and monotonous activity and works hard to make it more interesting and challenging.

6. The high achiever is *not* more motivated by individual than by group goals. The critical considerations are that the achievers be given clear feedback on their progress toward the goal and that successful attainment of the goal be recognized as virtuous by the group.

7. The high achiever is slightly more inclined to be responsive to admiring peers than he or she is to admiring authorities.

8. High achievers are not naturally drawn to business and economic pursuits. They are attracted to the difficulty of the task and by the community's belief that the task should be undertaken. In many countries the high achievers tend to be in the nonbusiness sectors. Among students at Ivy League schools in the United States, the high achievers of upper-middle-class backgrounds also were more attracted to the nonbusiness sectors of society. It was the high achievers of working-class and lower-middle-class backgrounds who were most inclined to feel challenged by and desirous of a business career.

In seeking solutions to the economic problems of the American poor of the twentieth century, particularly those of blacks in the urban ghettos, many have advocated the fostering of individual entrepreneurs as the key. The Office of Minority Business Enterprise of the Department of Commerce was established largely to do precisely this. However, an equally large group has asserted that such a program cannot possibly succeed, arguing that the absence of social institutions such as the extended family and a unified religious community preclude the development of enough entrepreneurs to make a meaningful difference for the whole community.[9] Others have contended that the emphasis upon integration and education for blacks and other minority groups effectively prevents the emergence of local entrepreneurs.[10] They reason that, having received decent educations, blacks and members of other minorities expect the rewards of relatively high salaries and job security. Entrepreneurial organizing seldom offers either reward very soon. Integration, too, they claim, tends to impede the development of black entrepreneurship, since minorities tend to be incorporated into existing white institutions, not the other way around. Hence there are fewer opportunities to be the initiators of new institutions, organizations, and projects.[11]

Geoffrey Faux has pointed out that even if a small number of individual entrepreneurs were to develop in the ghettos, they would be too isolated to be able to exert the influence required to deal with the complex political problems they would face.[12] To develop land in a city, for example, requires the approval of several layers of political associations and bureaucracies, if, for instance, zoning changes are needed. In addition, it is usually not possible to justify the special distribution of public funds to a select group of "entrepreneurs" if it requires discrimination on the basis of race.

C. M. Hampden-Turner, a research psychologist who has studied McClelland's findings, argues that sociological and psychological research on entrepreneurial achievement demonstrates that "the point of greatest leverage in developing an impoverished sector is to encourage the growth of communities oriented to achievement and development. Selecting individual entrepreneurs in the hope that they can galvanize their communities would probably be less successful."[13] In his judgment, so long as individual entrepreneurs represent an exception to the style and sentiment of the community, they will have little motivation to work for the community. If they are successful, which is rare, they will be more inclined to move out of the poor community, where few peers admire them, and into the dominant suburban society, where their peers will. Hampden-Turner also argues that "the achievement oriented community precedes rather than follows physically achieving persons" and that "a relatively egalitarian ethic oriented to community benefit and cooperation . . . [is] best designed to elicit achievement motivation."[14]

Entrepreneurship through Community Economic Development

According to the preceding discussion, then, it was the search for an effective method of fostering black capitalism and black entrepreneurs that led people to the rather socialistic-sounding solution of community economic development. The socialistic aspect is more apparent than real. In fact, two scholars have even stressed the great similarities that exist between the twentieth-century community development corporations and the three most significant joint-stock trading companies of the sixteenth century, the Virginia, Plymouth, and Massachusetts Bay Companies, the progenitors of both representative government and the publicly held business corporation in the United States.[15]

The stress on community in the community economic development program stems from the realization that community deterioration is not only physical but also institutional. It is based on the fact that the decision to participate in a community, to migrate from it, or to fall into apathy are alternative rational responses to the problem of community decline.[16] Each of these decisions has its own price in terms of energy, money, time, and choice of friends and type of social and physical environment. The people who have migrated from the deteriorating U.S. communities have been primarily those with the greatest leadership potential, both for maintaining community institutions and for becoming entrepreneurs. By addressing the institutional deterioration of the low-income communities and by building upon the new cultural awakening of the blacks, Chicanos, Indians, Puerto Ricans, and white ethnic groups, the community economic development program seeks to revivify the American entrepreneurial spirit in poverty environments. To a large extent the program assumes that ethnic or racial consciousness and neighborhood identity are the modern counterparts of the Protestant ethic and proud nationalism of earlier generations.[17]

The Relationship between Community
and Individual Entrepreneurship

To illustrate the relationship between community and individually focused efforts to foster capitalism and entrepreneurship and to highlight their similarities and differences, a comparison was made by Stewart E. Perry between the program concepts of the Title VII community economic development program of the Economic Opportunity Act and those of the minority entrepreneurship program of the Office of Minority Business Enterprise (OMBE) of the Department of Commerce.[18] This comparison shows the differences in definition of the problems to be solved, the framework for action, the strategic answers given, the measures of program success, and the program limitations.

Under Title VII the problem is defined as a community in trouble, the focus is on particular low-income communities, and action is taken to remedy those communities' needs. OMBE, on the other hand, defines the problem as a citizen in trouble; the focus is on the economically or socially disadvantaged individual, and action is taken in terms of that individual's needs.

The Title VII program seeks the strategic answer to the problem of poverty in increased strength in such community characteristics as the following:

1. Better planning, coordination, mobilization, and integration of existing resources.

2. Creation of new resources (or expansion of existing resources) in the three basic areas of social tools, human resources, and physical infrastructure.

The social tools (institutions) include such organizations as CDCs and cooperatives for coordination; businesses for production; banks and credit unions for financial resources; new political linkages for informing and influencing decision making; and police, and so on, for services. Human resources, at all levels and for various roles, are developed in terms of skills and of increased hopes, aspirations, and community loyalty. The physical infrastructure, of course, includes such items as roads, lighting, parks, and public buildings. The program provides flexible equity capital for investment in any of the three types of new resources or for expanding the existing resources of any of the basic types.

3.   Ownership by the community.

OMBE, in contrast, seeks the strategic answer in increased strength in individual characteristics, such as the following:

1.   Greater personal skills in such areas as management, accounting, and marketing, and/or
2.   Access to technical assistance or consultation to gain access to debt capital or markets for skills and the products of those skills.
3.   Ownership by an entrepreneur.

Under Title VII, program success is measured by a complex approach that requires weighted measures of the various components that together define a successful program. Among those components are the following:

1.   The number of new institutions. This includes business institutions, although viable businesses are only one type of possible institutional result.
2.   Greater diversification of the social tools (institutions) that enrich opportunities. This means that there should be not just more barber shops, but computer facilities and so on.
3.   An increase in the incomes of residents; income increases for nonresidents are not as relevant.
4.   Increased employment in upgraded jobs. The income from these jobs might not change, but the opportunity for better income might.
5.   An increase of incomes in the lower ranges, not just an average increase due to large advances in the upper ranges.
6.   An upgraded physical environment, with less pollution, more resources, and so on, to increase community attraction.
7.   Stability or an increase in net immigration of talent and skillls.
8.   Increased investments, especially equity investments by residents.

The OMBE measure of success is much simpler; this approach results in one easily identified measure of success; which is whether the citizen now owns and operates a viable business (or a larger-scale business).

These two contrasting programs have some major program limitations in common: both are vulnerable to and dependent upon broad national trends in fiscal and monetary policies. The Title VII program additionally involves high costs, since their objectives are ambitious. The Title VII approach is further handicapped by the multiple indicators necessary to measure its success (see above); any one of these indicators might look poor, even though the others look good; this makes defense of the program complex. The OMBE program, however, has a more serious deficiency, since it fails to deal with the community environment, which is a crucial element in individual chances of success.

As this comparison shows, the community economic development movement in no way opposes or contradicts the American tradition of individual entrepreneurship. Rather, it seeks to provide in a systematic way a community-based framework of institutional support so that not only will such entrepreneurship be nourished and brought to maturity, but also the community as a whole will benefit from the development of its own entrepreneurs.

THE GOALS OF COMMUNITY
ECONOMIC DEVELOPMENT

The Legislative Requirement

The goals of the community economic development program, both in legislation and in practice, are broad and all-encompassing.[19] The legislation specifies that the program is to seek appreciable, lasting solutions to the problems of low-income communities. In broad terms the needs to be addressed are poverty, chronic underemployment and unemployment, community deterioration, and dependency.

To alleviate the employment problems, the CDCs are expected to create and upgrade jobs in their communities. They are to establish new business ventures that will be stable and self-supporting. Through these ventures and related activities, the CDC is supposed to develop jobs for the previously unemployed and provide better-quality jobs with greater security and higher incomes for residents who are already employed.

In most poverty areas the creating and upgrading of jobs by the CDCs depends upon their effectiveness in reducing the physical and institutional deterioration of their communities. Thus the CDCs seek to provide for and to improve the community's infrastructure, that is, those services that contribute to successful economic development, such as water and sewer systems, transportation, and day-care centers. They seek to improve the physical environment by supporting organizations that rehabilitate houses, commercial and public facilities, and land and other natural resources. They also support organizations that construct new housing, shopping, and production facilities. They seek to offset the institutional deterioration of the community by forming new organizations, particularly business ventures, and by increasing the financial and technical support of community organization by the public and private sectors, that is, by government agencies and business and financial institutions. They also combat deterioration by directly fostering the development of the managerial and entrepreneurial skills of the local residents.

The reduction of community dependency upon outsiders and the development of vital working institutions within the community depend heavily upon the CDCs' efforts to increase resident ownership of businesses, land, housing, and other commercial and private facilities. The CDC program for community economic development is built on the assumption that permanent changes in poverty areas will not occur unless the community environment itself can be made hospitable to economic development. Institutional development, community control, and community ownership of property and resources are expected to foster, support, and sustain the development of managerial and entrepreneurial leadership within the community—and to keep it there. In turn these changes are expected to provide the community with the human and institutional resources necessary to absorb and maintain the economic development process.

The legislation also requires that the CDCs have an "appreciable impact" upon their communities. While the meaning of "appreciable impact" is open to considerable debate, for urban areas the impact of the program has tended to be evaluated by comparing the progress in the impact area of the CDC with that of the entire metropolitan area. In rural areas the point of comparison with the CDC target area is the state. According to one of the monitors of the $2 million evaluation of the CDC program in 1970-72, the following ought to be taken into account in the evaluation:

> The definitions of both the expected amount of impact on community problems and the necessary time for that impact should be consistent with each other and with (a) the magnitude of problems in the SIP [Special Impact Program] areas and the extent of the difference between the Impact and surrounding areas, (b) the amount and duration of SIP funds going to each CDC, (c) the amount of private and public funds leveraged by SIP funds, and (d) the number, resources, and stability of other community organizations in the Impact area with activities and objectives that are complementary with the SIP.[20]

The legislative requirement that CDCs have "appreciable impact" did not take into account the internal politics of the Office of Economic Opportunity; nor did it recognize that OEO and its programs, includng the CDC program, would become political footballs. During the heyday of Howard Phillips as Director of OEO, when the dismantling of OEO and its programs was the prime target, estimates of the time and funds needed to achieve "appreciable impact" were not based on the most rational criteria. It is undeniable that the purposes of many governmental programs are altered somewhat during their actual execution. Nonetheless, the original conception of the community economic development program had—and still does have—a reasonable approach, through which the federal government contributes to helping the CDCs reach their goals.

As the CDC program was first designed, the federal government was to fund each CDC for 15 years. Funds allocated during the first 10 years were to be used for investment and administrative capital; during the next 5 years the funds were to be used primarily for administrative purposes, to enable ventures that had been started by the CDC to achieve a fully self-supporting status.[21] In practice, however, OEO gave the CDCs only two-year grants, renewable at OEO's option, in order to maintain control and to ensure that the legislative requirements and standards were met.

An additional problem for the CDCs seeking to attain "appreciable impact" is the amount of funds OEO had at its disposal. From the time the program began in fiscal 1968, through fiscal 1974, OEO had spent about $106 million on the community economic development program.[22] Although this amount had considerable leverage on the whole, it is a very small sum for such a large task. If, for instance, you were to divide the $106 million equally among the 35 CDCs included in this study, each would get less than $3 million. One CDC, however, the Bedford-Stuyvesant Restoration Corporation in Brooklyn, New York, has received about $33 million, or roughly one-third, of this total amount, and a few others, like the North Lawndale CDC in Chicago, Illinois, have received over $10 million; as a consequence, the average for most CDCs is much closer to $1.5 million. That, of course, is not much money for fighting a war on poverty, even if the target area is "only" a part of a large inner city.

The Title VII legislation also requires that the community economic development programs bring permanent changes to their target communities. Although the precise means of making both "appreciable" and "permanent" impacts are left to the CDCs and their governing boards, one planner at OEO has suggested that this requirement indicated that OEO should encourage the following priorities for the use of OEO funds:

1. the establishment of stable and continuing organizations to foster and sustain long-term economic growth;

2. the use of funds primarily in ventures and organizations that produce goods and services that yield revenue and that can be self-supporting after funding terminates;

3. the use of funds for land and housing and for commercial, industrial, and public facilities that yield a flow of services over time; and

4. minimal use of funds for activities yielding benefits for one point in time and activities in which there is no provision for replacement of services used or maintenance of the flow of benefits.[23]

Practical Results of the Legislation

Sooner or later the legislative goals and requirements of the federal bureaucracy must be met by people at the local level. Because the CDC program relies heavily upon the community control concept, each CDC, in the form of its governing board of directors, is charged with the responsibility for setting the specific objectives of its community economic development program. Although the objectives of each CDC are individualized, there are general objectives that all CDCs have in common. During the Kelly survey, the board members were asked to select what in their opinion were the top three most important objectives for a community economic development program. They were given eleven specific objectives from which to choose and an option to specify others. Table 2.1 shows the relative ranking the choices received from the 273 respondents.

The responses of the CDC board members appear to stress the means of achieving the OEO national goals more than than the end goals themselves. To illustrate, the goal of reducing unemployment can be addressed by means of creating jobs and profitable businesses; but it is not usually possible to create jobs and profitable businesses by reducing unemployment. In other words, by the time the problem of defining goals reaches the CDC boards, the focus of attention is the means of reaching the broader nationally established goals of the program, not on what the basic nature and scope of the goals should be.

Like the board members, the chairpersons of the CDC boards of directors also tended to place greatest importance upon creating jobs, with 53 percent selecting this as one of the three most important objectives. (See Table 2.2.) Providing opportunities for community-controlled ownership of businesses and property ranks a close second, however, over developing profitable businesses, which was the board members' second choice.

The executive directors as a group most frequently chose providing opportunities for community-controlled ownership of businesses and property (65 percent), creating jobs (60 percent), and developing profitable businesses (60 percent) as their three most important goals. (See Table 2.3.) As a group, the directors apparently see a much closer relationship among these three objectives than either the board chairpersons or the members. Neither the board members nor the board chairpersons stress developing profitable businesses as much as the directors do.

Rural-Urban Differences

Given the difference in the nature of poverty in rural and urban areas, one would expect that the geographical location of the CDC would have a

TABLE 2.1

The Three Most Important Objectives of Community Economic Development:
Board Members in Kelly Survey
(N = 273)

| Objectives | Percent Ranking Item | | | | Total Percent |
	First	Second	Third	Checked*	Selecting Item
Creating jobs	30	14	8	8	60
Developing profitable businesses	17	14	6	3	40
Reducing unemployment	7	7	12	4	30
Providing manpower training and development	7	10	8	3	28
Providing opportunities for local individual ownership of businesses and property	4	11	10	3	28
Providing opportunities for community-controlled ownership of businesses and property	13	12	7	3	35
Reducing community deterioration (developing land, resources, and property)	9	11	8	2	30
Reducing community dependence on outsiders	1	4	7	2	14
Increasing incomes of those already employed	0	1	2	2	5
Reducing number of people leaving the area	0	4	8	2	14
Getting outside institutions to aid in community development	2	2	8	2	14

*The "checked" column represents respondents who did not choose among the top three goals by ranking them; several persons just checked the most important goals. Some also checked more than three items. So as not to lose this information, the data are presented under the "checked" column.
Source: The author's 1973 survey of CDC board members.

TABLE 2.2

The Three Most Important Objectives of Community Economic Development: Board Chairpersons in Kelly Survey
(N = 19)

Objectives	Percent Ranking Item			Total Percent Selecting Item
	First	Second	Third	
Creating jobs	11	16	26	53
Developing profitable businesses	21	5	5	31
Reducing unemployment	11	11	0	22
Providing manpower training and development	0	0	11	11
Providing opportunities for local individual ownership of businesses and property	5	16	0	21
Providing opportunities for community-controlled ownership of businesses and property	21	16	11	48
Reducing community deterioration (developing land, resources, and property)	11	21	5	37
Reducing community dependence on outsiders	0	0	11	11
Increasing incomes of those already employed	0	0	0	0
Reducing number of people leaving the area	5	5	0	10
Getting outside institutions to aid in community development	5	0	11	16

Source: The author's 1973 survey of CDC chairpersons.

TABLE 2.3

The Three Most Important Objectives of Community Economic Development: Executive Directors in Kelly Survey
(N = 20)

Objectives	Percent Ranking Item			Total Percent
	First	Second	Third	Selecting Item
Creating jobs	15	30	15	60
Developing profitable businesses	20	25	15	60
Reducing unemployment	5	10	10	25
Providing manpower training and development	0	0	10	10
Providing opportunities for local individual ownership of businesses and property	5	5	5	15
Providing opportunities for community-controlled ownership of businesses and property	40	10	15	65
Reducing community deterioration (developing land, resources, and property)	5	15	5	25
Reducing community dependence on outsiders	0	0	0	0
Increasing incomes of those already employed	0	0	5	5
Reducing number of people leaving the area	5	5	15	25
Getting outside institutions to aid in community development	5	0	5	10

Source: The author's 1973 survey of CDC executive directors.

great influence on the specific objectives set for it by its board, and that is indeed the case. Rural board members place much greater emphasis on creating jobs, and they are much more agreed among themselves that this objective is the most important goal of a community economic development program. Of the rural members, 69 percent, compared to 51 percent of the urban members, selected this objective as one of the three most important. They also placed greater stress on reducing unemployment (39 percent, compared to 24 percent of the urban members) and on reducing the number of people leaving their target areas (22 percent, compared to 10 percent of the urban members). Reducing community deterioration, that is, developing land, resources, and property, is emphasized by the urban members significantly more than by the rural members (42 percent to 12 percent).

The chairpersons did not vary so sharply by geographical location. Only on the objective of reducing community deterioration did a substantial difference appear. While 60 percent of the urban chairpersons placed this objective among the three most important for a community economic development program, only 11 percent of the rural chairpersons did.

Differences by Amount of Funds Received from the Office of Economic Opportunity in Fiscal 1968 and Fiscal 1974. The goals set for the various CDCs do not appear to be related to the amounts of funds the CDCs have received.

Goals of Specific Community Development Corporations

It is obvious from the general statistics presented that at the local level the CDC governing boards have stayed quite close to the national legislative requirements. Most of the variations in objectives can be accounted for in terms of variations in the situation of the CDC communities. This can best be illustrated by general descriptions of several specific CDCs.[24]

Community Development Corporations Serving Rural Areas

The rural CDCs are spread throughout the country, serving Indian tribes, blacks, Chicanos, and various white ethnic groups. The collective scope of these CDCs is quite broad. The Lummi Indian Tribal Enterprises (LITE) CDC in Marietta, Washington, which is the chartered business development arm of the Lummi Indian Business Council, serves as the management body for economic development on the Lummi Indian reservation. This CDC has concentrated most of the more than $2 million it has received from OEO into obtaining equity in and leverage for a variety of aquaculture projects: a fish hatchery, an oyster hatchery, and a massive seapond constructed on 750 acres of Lummi tidelands.

About 140 people, mostly Lummis, were employed to build these plants, and to operate them another 100 were trained with Department of Labor Manpower Development Training Act funds. When possible, local Lummi construction contractors were used.

Standing Rock Industries in Fort Yates, North Dakota, serves the Standing Rock Sioux reservation. It has concentrated on the problems of unemployment, housing, and limited commercial services by starting business ventures such as a manufacturing firm to produce low-cost modular housing, a coin-operated laundromat, a firm to deliver bulk propane gas, and retail grocery stores. Almost all the people employed by the CDC were on welfare before. This CDC operates within the context of a 30-year master plan developed for the reservation by the Sioux tribal council.

Impact Seven, Incorporated, which started partly through the efforts of its U.S. Senator, Gaylord Nelson, serves seven counties in northwestern Wisconsin, including two Chippewa Indian reservations. Since its inception in July 1970, the CDC has received funds or assistance from the Economic Development Administration (EDA), the Small Business Administration (SBA), the Bureau of Indian Affairs (BIA), the U.S. Department of Housing and Urban Development (HUD), the Farmers Home Administration (FHA), the State OEO, the State Division of Economic Development, the University of Wisconsin, and the State Department of Local Affairs and Development. By 1972 it had been able to influence "the acquisition of property valued at $3,424,000 for residential, agricultural and social use, and the development of property worth $39,000."[25]

The Midwest Minnesota CDC in Detroit Lakes, Minnesota, serves a predominantly white population and a few (about 3 percent) White Earth Indians. It has tended to stress ventures that can use land and timber, the major natural resources in the area, although it has also formed a potato processing plant and a cooperative for marketing crops at roadside stands. Its major strategy is to create local markets for local supplies. Creating jobs as such is less important.

Other rural CDCs serve predominantly Spanish-speaking populations; the Siete del Norte (SDN) CDC in Espanola, New Mexico, is one of these. SDN has, among other things, stressed improvement of the organization and marketing of apple production and cattle. It has also supported manufacturing ventures producing wood products and furniture. The Adela Development Corporation in Salt Lake City, Utah, also serves a large Spanish-speaking population. It directs its efforts to providing employment for migrant laborers and seasonal farm workers who have decided to settle in more urban areas. Its chief goal is "to facilitate the transition of the target population from participation in the rural agrarian economy to the urban industrial economy." Because of the skills of its target population, Adela has concentrated on a janitorial venture.

Rural CDCs also serve predominantly black target areas. Examples of these include Seminole Employment and Economic Development Corporation (SEEDCO), based in Sanford, Florida; the Southeast Alabama CDC (SACDC), based in Troy, Alabama; and the Delta Foundation based in Greenville,

Mississippi. SEEDCO was developed by the residents of the largely black rural population of Seminole County in central Florida. Because of their past work experience in farming and farm-related work, the poor in this area find it difficult to compete with the incoming skilled and semiskilled workers for nonfarm jobs. To combat this competitive disadvantage, SEEDCO has been starting and operating ventures such as Semsan Nursery, which grows plants, provides landscaping services, and sells its nursery products retail.

The SACDC serves Pike, Bullock, and Cook counties. It seeks to reduce unemployment by supporting ventures that will bring together the abundant lumber in the area with the unskilled labor. Midway Wood Products, a manufacturing company, has been its main venture. Another venture, the PBC Construction company, buys prefabricated homes, prepares homesites for erection, and then erects the homes. The total cost of the house to the buyer is about $13,000, which still leaves the company with a small profit. Through such work, this CDC is making visible contributions to the betterment of its target population's standard of living while simultaneously giving employment to some of that same population.

The Delta Foundation serves 14 counties in the rural Mississippi delta. It seeks to improve the situation of its predominantly black population by operating a plant for cutting and sewing blue jeans that employs about 75 people, most of them low skilled and low paid. By exporting the blue jeans through its marketing subsidiary, the Delta Sales Corporation, Delta hopes to bring outside funds into the area for further capital investment. Delta's efforts were responsible for the shift of the Mid-South Metal Stamping Company from Memphis, Tennessee, to Sardis, Mississippi; this provides the region with another labor-intensive firm for jobs and the capital from a highly exportable product. Between fiscal 1970 and fiscal 1972, this CDC leveraged fifty cents from the private sector for every OEO dollar, or over an additional $1 million.

Community Development Corporations Serving Urban Areas

The urban CDCs vary perhaps even more than the rural CDCs in their scope and objectives. A description of a few of the 21 included in the 1973-74 OEO program will suggest the range of their activities.

There are no urban Indian CDCs, and there is only one white ethnic one— the East Boston CDC. It serves a predominantly Italian-American population of 39,000 living near Boston's Logan International Airport. The major problem this CDC seeks to address is the decline in population and in business and manufacturing firms in the area, as well as housing deterioration. Unlike most of the other CDCs, East Boston has not stressed creating jobs, but rather has focused on long-range housing and commercial waterfront development plans.

The black CDCs in urban areas range in size from the very large, long-established Bedford–Stuyvesant Restoration Corporation in Brooklyn, New

York, which has received over $33 million of OEO funds to date, to much smaller efforts that have involved less than $1 million from OEO.

The Bedford-Stuyvesant CDC serves over 450,000 people in an extremely overcrowded section of Brooklyn. At the time of the CDC's inception, the area had a very high crime rate, massive unemployment, and a very deteriorated physical base. While many of the problems remain, the CDC, according to an independent evaluator, has created, or contributed to the creation of, several thousand jobs and is the CDC that has come closest "to achieving an annual job creation which would eliminate official unemployment in ten years."[26] Through its efforts, an IBM plant and branch offices of Chemical Bank, Consolidated Edison, and Metropolitan Life, as well as several other such companies, have located in the area. Bedford-Stuyvesant's community development targets have mainly been in the area of property development and improvement of housing. It has constructed or helped to construct several large apartment buildings, ranging in size from fifty to several hundred units; it has rehabilitated several hundred other housing units internally; and it has renovated several hundred more externally. Land has also been obtained and cleared for additional housing and commercial development. The large Sheffield Center, a former dairy complex, has been completely rehabilitated and another large commercial center adjacent to it is being built. The CDC has also been active in outreach programs operating from its neighborhood centers and in cultural affairs, having built, for example, the Billie Holiday Theater in the Sheffield Center, as a focus for the arts.

The Hough Area Development Corporation and the North Lawndale Economic Development Corporation (NLEDC), the former in Cleveland, Ohio, and the latter in Chicago, Illinois, are also large CDCs, each having received over $10 million in OEO funds between fiscal 1968 and fiscal 1974. Hough covers the predominantly black part of Cleveland. Development here has concentrated on the Martin Luther King Plaza, a retail food store, two retail fast-food stores, a manufacturing venture, and a service handyman maintenance firm. The Great Eastern Holding Company, a wholly owned subsidiary of the CDC, is the means by which community ownership of these ventures and properties is implemented. Property development and the construction of housing units, such as the Homes for Hough activities, are directed toward reducing community deterioration and instilling pride of community and ownership.

NLEDC has a much more narrowly focused development program. Its primary goal is physical redevelopment of the target area; thus activities center on the large-scale, highly visible development of a shopping center and an industrial park.[27] It also has a management training and internship program for preparing local residents for operating the new ventures connected with the shopping center and the industrial park.

Two CDCs, United Durham, Incorporated (UDI), in North Carolina and the Circle in Boston, Massachusetts, provide examples of the goals of CDCs that have had less than $2 million of support from OEO and are serving black populations. UDI seeks to develop managerial and technical skills and to increase community capabilities, essentially by means of the operation of a modular homes manufacturing firm and a supermarket. Community ownership is stressed, as well as the delivery of goods, services, and housing.

The Circle serves the predominantly black communities of Roxbury, the South End, and Dorchester in Boston. To spread its influence and to reach the intended beneficiaries, the Circle works through precinct and neighborhood development corporations in its area. In addition to starting at least two manufacturing firms, the Circle has been important in the development of the $2-million Boston Urban Capital company, which will be a major source of funds for local minority business entrepreneurs. It is also stressing the launching of more retail, service, and franchise ventures in its area, as well as real estate development.

Spanish-speaking populations also have CDCs in urban areas. The Denver CDC in Colorado and the Mexican-American Unity Council (MAUC) in San Antonio, Texas, are two of these. The Denver CDC serves about 100,000 people. Its plans are described as follows:

> Its intention to establish new community-owned businesses is phased in a three-part program. Within three years after becoming operational the CDC plans include the establishment of three large and six small businesses. Within five years after becoming operational, DCDC foresees the need to create an industrial park, a shopping center, two financial institutions, an equity loan fund for small businesses, and a chain store venture including a series of supermarkets and a single distribution center.[28]

Although the Denver CDC did not receive OEO funds until July 1970, its Adelante Community Supermarket was at a financial break-even point by mid-1972.

The target population of the Mexican-American Unity Council is about 300,000, of whom 84 percent are Mexican-Americans. This San Antonio area has a high proportion of teen-agers, broken homes, and related employment problems. MAUC's strategy has been to stress the development of as many Chicano-controlled small businesses as possible, with some development of franchises of well-known, name-brand firms. Ventures operating or being planned under MAUC influence or control include a McDonald's fast-food franchise, a bookkeeping company, a wholesale meat processor, and a retail supermarket. Longer-term community development plans involve construction of office buildings, shopping centers, a savings and loan company, a bank, and a mortgage and insurance company. This CDC also attempts to provide low-cost and improved housing.

CONCLUSION

As this brief and relatively general review of the CDC goals shows, the community economic development movement fits well into the American tradition of pulling oneself up by one's bootstraps. It differs from past efforts at encouraging entrepreneurship in that it is the community in these poverty environments, represented by its Community Development Corporation, that first seeks to identify, develop, foster, and nourish individual entrepreneurs and then to use their skills to develop the community further. In the past the individual entrepreneur was often seen as the initiator of the whole development acitivity: if the community benefited, fine; if not, too bad.

This community entrepreneurship also differs from past experience in the stress placed upon community ownership and control of economic development and businesses in these areas. While individual ownership of businesses and industry within these communities is supported, explicit concern is expressed, in practice as well as in theory, for keeping the benefits of this business activity within the target community. Community control, and not private, individual control, of resources and assets is one of the essential differences between its community entrepreneurship in poverty environments and previous entrepreneurial activity.

NOTES

1. Perhaps the best exposition of the role of the entrepreneur in capitalist development is given by the Austrian-born Harvard University economist, Joseph Schumpeter, in *The Theory of Economic Development*, trans. Redvers Opie (New York: Oxford University Press, 1961); the original German version appeared in 1909. See also Joseph Schumpeter, *Capitalism, Socialism, and Democracy*, 3rd ed. (New York: Harper & Row, 1962). Paul A. Samuelson employs the essence of Schumpeter's ideas in his basic economic textbook, *Economics: An Introductory Analysis* (New York: McGraw-Hill, 1951), which has been in use by most colleges and universities in the United States for over a decade.

2. The authors and scholars probing these areas are too numerous to list. For the context of this discussion, see Robert A. Nisbet, *The Quest for Community* (New York: Oxford University Press, 1953).

3. Max Weber, *The Protestant Ethnic and the Spirit of Capitalism* (London: Allen & Unwin, 1930).

4. Elliott D. Sclar, *The Community Basis of Economic Development* (Cambridge, Mass.: Center for Community Economic Development, 1970).

5. Richard Sennett, *Families Against the City: Middle Class Homes of Industrial Chicago, 1872-1890* (Cambridge: Harvard University Press, 1970).

6. Sclar, *The Community Basis*, p. 21.

7. Ivan H. Light, *Ethnic Enterprise in America: Business and Welfare Among Chinese, Japanese, and Blacks* (Berkeley: University of California Press, 1972).

8. David C. McClelland, *The Achieving Society* (Princeton: Van Nostrand, 1961).

9. Sclar, *The Community Basis*, p. 21.

10. Burt Griffin and Zachary Paris, unpublished manuscript, Chapter 16, p. 12 (available from the Center for Community Economic Development, Cambridge, Mass.).

11. This point is also found in ibid., Chapter 16, p. 12.

12. Geoffrey Faux, *CDCs: New Hope* (New York: Twentieth Century Fund, 1971).

13. C. M. Hampden-Turner, "The Myths and the Realities of Economic Achievement: The Importance of the Community," mimeographed (Cambridge, Mass.: Center for Community Economic Development, n.d.), p. 7.

14. Ibid., p. 6.

15. Patricia M. Lines and John McClaughry, *Early American Community Development Corporations: The Trading Companies* (Cambridge, Mass.: Center for Community Economic Development, 1970).

16. For a systematic analysis of this problem, see Albert O. Hirschman, *Exit, Voice, and Loyalty: Responses to Decline in Firms, Organizations, and States* (Cambridge: Harvard University Press, 1970).

17. In a manuscript in progress to which I have had access, Burt Griffin and Zachary Paris make this same point.

18. This comparison was prepared by Stewart E. Perry and first published in *CCED Newsletter* (February 1973).

19. See Title VII of the Economic Opportunity Amendments of 1972 (Public Law 92-424, September 19, 1972).

20. John M. Brazzel, "Design and Implementation of the OEO Special Impact Program (SIP) by the Office of Economic Development," draft manuscript, March 1, 1972, pp. 17-18.

21. Ibid., pp. 17-19.

22. Brian J. Reilly, "Distribution of SIP Funds." *CCED Newsletter*, February 1973.

23. Brazzel, "Design and Implementation," p. 26.

24. Descriptions of the objectives of the various CDCs are available to the public in such published documents as the Abt evaluation report, *An Evaluation of the Special Impact Program: Interim Report*, vol. 3, (Cambridge, Mass.: Abt Associates, 1973), especially in Chapter 15, "Analysis of 30 Grantees." Cast studies are available through the Center for Community Economic Development, which also maintains a special documents file on each CDC.

25. Abt report, *Interim Report*, vol. 3, Chapter 15, p. 10.

26. Ibid., Chapter 2, p. 29.

27. Ibid., Chapter 22, p. 1.

28. Ibid., Chapter 8, p. 1.

3

COMMUNITY ENTREPRENEURSHIP
AND CONTROL BY WHOM?

The outcry against the massive public clearance projects and urban renewal programs of the 1950s and early 1960s and the riots of the late 1960s gave the impetus needed to bring resident-controlled community development corporations into being. The government and public wanted to see that public monies actually benefited the intended beneficiaries. It would be necessary to solve the local political problems involved in land acquisition, tenant relocation, rezoning, and business development in the ghetto; the fact that in many poor areas racial hostility, lack of safety, and lack of profits had driven away private developers led to the conclusion that without resident and community participation no progress would be made.

What does the word "community" in community economic development mean? Who in any community controls or at least sits on the governing boards of the community development corporations? To what extent can these governing boards be considered legitimate representatives of their communities?

WHAT IS A COMMUNITY?

The General OEO View

The word "community" has many different actual and possible political, economic, ideological, social, and other meanings; efforts to define it precisely inevitably fail to satisfy some faction. Prior to the riots in Watts, Hough, and other ghetto areas of large cities, the word "community" was almost never applied to neighborhoods or blocks in cities. Instead it was usually used to denote a population (1) that was territorially organized, (2) that was more or less completely rooted in the soil it occupied, and (3) in which the individual units functioned in a relationship of mutual interdependence. This three-pronged definition of community is largely a holdover of the Chicago school of sociology and community studies from the time of World War II and before. Because community studies fell into disfavor in the late 1940s and 1950s, most Americans and their politicians seem to have kept it as a working definition long after its relationship to reality had ended.[1]

Even Robert Kennedy, who was a major factor in the development of OEO and other programs pushing for community participation, tended to view the community in this way. To him the community consisted of a coalition of social, business, religious, welfare, industrial, governmental, voluntary, and private interests. Their interdependence required the groups and interests to act together as a "community."[2] The original OEO legislation did not refer to any administrative unit smaller than a town or city.[3]

The riots and OEO's experience between 1964 and 1966 led Congress to realize that traditional political entities were insufficient for an effective war on poverty. Hence Section 202(a) of the Economic Opportunity Act was amended in 1966 to permit Community Action Programs in "any neighborhood or other area (irrespective of boundaries or political subdivisions) which is sufficiently homogeneous in character to be an appropriate area for an attack on poverty under this part."[4]

In 1967 the passage of the Green Amendment, which required that local public officials have one-third of the seats on the boards of directors of all Community Action Agencies, appeared to nullify the new neighborhood definition of community.[5] The nullification, however, was more in appearance than in reality. While it is indeed true that mayors were given increased citywide control over OEO local programs, the control did not extent to actual operations. OEO began to require that local neighborhood advisory boards incorporate for the purpose of receiving contracts for program implementation. Through incorporation the neighborhoods once again received resident control over budgets, personnel, and OEO programs operating in their areas.[6]

The Office of Economic Opportunity Program View of Community Development Corporations

In 1968 and 1969, when the Special Impact Program that was setting up the community economic development program at OEO was still in its early stages, the definition of community was already accepted, as was the use of a neighborhood-resident-controlled corporation for implementing programs. Hence no new effort was made to redefine "community." The areas to receive OEO funds under the program were defined by their poverty characteristics: predominance of low-income families, underemployment and unemployment, high-density population, and high crime rate. In other words, the definition of community has been and is still based essentially upon the needs and deficiencies of the neighborhood.

Adequacy of the Current Definition

The OEO program definition of a Community Development Corporation is most certainly *not* based on either an everyday or a social science usage of the term. As Robert Nisbet has pointed out, "community" refers to ties "characterized by a high degree of personal intimacy, emotional depth, moral commitment, social cohesion, and continuity in time."[7] Most low-income neighborhoods exist simply as the result of their spatial contiguity. Social scientists have tended to define "neighborhoods" without reference to the concept of "community" at all. According to Suzanne Keller, four different definition exist, based on natural geographic boundaries, on evidence as to the uses of neighborhood facilities, on the cultural characteristics of the residents, and on resident perceptions.[8]

The approach of the CDC program of OEO to defining "community" by negative criteria obviously limits what is meant by "community economic development." Although no theory of community economic development has yet been articulated, it is apparent that something different from the traditional types of economic development is being attempted. The stress on community would suggest that this development is building upon the positive, cohesive characteristics of the localities in question, but what these positive features are has not yet been spelled out. A more adequate definition will undoubtedly be developed as more research is completed.

Sometimes in the initial stages of the organization of a CDC, the geographical definition of community, and hence of potential participants in the CDC, is not followed, Instead, ethnic identity may be the criterion. This can be understood in the light of the history of discrimination against blacks, Chicanos, and native American Indians and of the strong identity movements that have arisen in response to discrimination and to successes in the civil rights movement. Thus, for example a black economic development group, later funded by OEO, originally restricted its membership to local blacks. This group, like any that seeks federal funding, had to change its bylaws before getting grant support.[9] Mostly, however, it is possible for a rural or even an urban CDC to stake out its constituency simply on the basis of a poverty-level income and thereby pretty much appeal to, and be responded to by, a single ethnic or racial group within its target area.*

---

*Of course, census figures for the target areas demonstrate that concentration in black ghettos, Spanish barrios, and Indian reservation lands. These figures are often cited in the proposals for Title VII support which must also include the percentage of poverty-level residents, which makes the target area eligible.

OEO often places a special condition on CDC grants requiring that membership in the CDC be open to all target-area residents. OEO- and CSA- funded CDCs, theoretically at least, therefore, have open access to membership for all residents of the communities they serve. Today the membership of most governing boards is chosen by the larger membership or by community-based organizations, which in turn are usually open to all community residents.

PARTICIPATION OF THE "COMMUNITY" IN THE COMMUNITY DEVELOPMENT CORPORATION

The phrase "community economic development" and the geographical emphasis in the legislation authorizing the community economic development program suggest that all the people in a given area are eligible for active participation in a local CDC. In practice this has never been so. Participation and, through that, control, is not an automatic right of residency. The CDC member is usually a recognized part of the existing leadership in the neighborhood.[10] The constitutional bylaws of a CDC govern its operation, and in the beginning these bylaws are almost always the private conception of a few individuals, the enterprising entrepreneurs, if you will, who have the vision and energy to create an economic development institution in a low-income area.

Membership Eligibility

The legal structure of each CDC and the bylaws in that structure determine who is eligible for membership, what the obligations of membership are, how large the board of directors shall be, and how many members are to be selected to serve on it. The particular legal structure of the CDC will naturally vary with the specific purposes that have led to its formation. There are non-profit, for-profit, and cooperative community development corporations. The nonprofit corporation, the usual form for CDCs, is a legal entity formed to advance broad social goals or charitable purposes, such as that of aiding a community's economic development. Like the membership eligibility requirements, these goals and statements of purpose are included in the CDC's bylaws, which are registered with the state.

Most CDCs with the nonprofit legal form are open to all residents within their defined geographical areas. Occasionally, however, income limitations are imposed, to assure than low-income people will be the main participating group. The boards of directors that are to control the CDCs are selected either directly or indirectly from the members of community organizations. Personal financial gain may be realized through the stocks and profits of wholly owned subsidiaries of the CDC. Under the OEO administrative rules, board members of the CDCs are not permitted compensation for their services, though they may be reimbursed for out-of-pocket expenses for travel to meetings, for babysitters during time away from home, and so on. This sometimes means that a board member will resign his or her position in order to take a paying job within the CDC or one of its subsidiaries.

The nonprofit CDC is popular because it permits tax-exempt status, the receiving of grant funds from foundations and governmental agencies, and the separate incorporation of businesses wholly owned by the nonprofit corporation. This latter possibility prevents the creditors of one business from reaching the assets and profits of another, thus shielding the profitable businesses launched by the CDC from the failing ventures. Separate incorporation also makes it easier to sell some or all of the stock of the separate businesses to community residents when the businesses become sufficiently successful. This legal structure usually requires the smallest initial overt commitment from residents who desire membership in the CDC.

The for-profit corporation is a legal entity formed specifically to conduct businesses for stockholders—its only members. They in turn choose the board of directors. This type of corporation is used by some CDCs because it permits them to engage in political activities, which are often necessary if major land developments are contemplated. It also allows for pooling of the profits and losses of the CDC's subsidiaries for tax purposes. It attracts investments, in contrast to the contributions usually received by the nonprofit CDCs, and it permits the distribution of dividends. This form is particularly helpful if the CDC often deals with the Small Business Administration (SBA), which does not recognize nonprofit corporations as small businesses.

The for-profit CDC is not as popular as the nonprofit CDC, largely for psychological reasons: in the United States, for-profit corporations usually do not have the reputation of being run in the public interest. Furthermore, one must choose to be a stockholder, not just a resident of the community, to be a member. It is also difficult and risky to sell stock to low-income people, particularly when immediate profits cannot be anticipated. In addition, as the multipurpose, comprehensive planning organization for a community, it is preferable that the CDC be able to receive tax-exempt contributions and to maintain its reputation as a community entity quite different from that of just another business organization.

The cooperative corporation is most popular in rural areas, where farmers are familiar with this legal structure. It is chosen if the community plans to market home-grown or homemade products and to share the profits according to each person's output. To belong, a person must usually produce or consume a specific product as well as reside within a specific target area. The main advantage of this legal entity is that earnings are taxed only once, as the income of the individual member. Most corporations must pay taxes on the organization's profits; then the stockholders pay on their earnings as well. CDCs do not usually take the form of cooperatives because many states restrict the functions cooperatives may perform. Although one CDC with the cooperative legal structure is briefly described in this chapter, none are included in the Abt and Kelly data.

Membership Obligations

Some CDCs have specific written obligations that their members must meet. Attendance requirements at major meetings are used by several CDCs to eliminate curiosity-seekers and nonworkers. Other CDCs have financial obligations for membership, either membership fees or the purchase of voting stock. Because the financial returns on CDC ventures are not yet a reality in most cases, the difference between these two types of financial obligation is minimal.

The reasons for these financial obligations are both historical and ideological. Early advocates of the program, particularly Robert Kennedy, felt that CDCs could and would provide a means for low-income residents to gain a stake in the country's economy. Through stock ownership and financial participation in the CDC, poor people would eventually gain self-sufficiency. The opportunity to participate in the economy like the middle and upper classes who invest in the stock and bond markets was also seen as a means of fostering pride. This in turn led to the assumption among some planners than an important success indicator of the OEO-funded CDCs should be the proportion of low-income residents owning CDC stock. in May 1972, however, a task force of CDC leaders recommended that stock ownership not be used as an indicator of community participation.[11] Even the most aggressive efforts at selling low-cost stock rights and memberships had produced participation of only 1 to 2 percent of the target population, or 5 to 10 percent of the family units. Those who took advantage of the ownership privilege tended to be the homeowners, the long-established residents, and the civic leaders of the community. The young radicals and the welfare activists have not tended to join CDCs except to exercise power as representatives of their organizations.

THE GOVERNING BOARDS OF COMMUNITY DEVELOPMENT CORPORATIONS: REPRESENTATIVES OF THEIR COMMUNITIES

The communities the CDCs serve range in size from a few thousand (for example, the Lummi Indian Tribe in the state of Washington) to several hundred thousand (for example, Bedord-Stuyvesant in Brooklyn, New York). In no case is direct democratic control of the CDC possible: the size of the communities and the CDC membership is too large. Hence the CDC boards of directors are the representatives of their communities and the focal points both for community input into the CDCs and control over the CDCs.

Sizes of the Governing Boards

The size of the governing board is obviously critical in terms of the effectiveness of its decision making and the control the community has over the

CDC administrative leadership. The size of governing boards in the private sector provides a point of comparison. A 1971 study of the boards of directors of manufacturing, mining, and retailing comanies, by Myles L. Mace, found that the average board had 15 members.[12] According to a 1961 study of 592 manufacturing companies surveyed by the National Industrial Conference Board, over 80 percent had an average of 11 members on their boards of directors.[13] This small size is considered conducive to increased participation and more effective decision making. The business concerns that had larger governing boards usually were institutions with a special interest in public relations and a need to attract and hold broad-based accounts.

The average size of the governing boards of the OEO-funded CDCs in the continental United States in 1973 was 17.[14] This figure is considerably higher than the average of 11 found for the 592 companies, but not much greater than the figure of 15 reported by Mace. The rural boards average 15 members, while the urban boards average 20 members. One might think that the greater ease of transportation in urban areas would tend to increase the size of the governing boards, that more people might be willing and able to participate than in rural areas; but the data do not support this assumption. (See Chapter 4.) Instead, their larger size is caused by the fact that they have more diverse interest groups and organizations, which need to be included in order to stabilize the CDC and give it legitimacy in the community.

The actual impact of the governing board's size on decision making and effective control over the CDC is not known. Boards with over 20 members will undoubtedly tend to have fewer people actively participating in meetings, simply because seating arrangements and time restraints force a teacher-student, leader-follower setting on the meetings, with discussions degenerating into reports from staff or committee leaders. The fact that the *average* number of board members for the urban CDCs is 20 suggests that these CDCs tend to have a subgroup within the board that becomes the effective decision-making body.

Several factors affect the size of a CDC board of directors. The membership eligibility requirements are basic. For instance, a CDC with closed membership that is limited to persons holding positions on the board must have a large board if new interest groups and individuals considered important for the CDC's progress are to be included. Because there is no other way to become a member, expansion of membership will necessarily lead to a large board. This type of closed membership once led the Hough Area Development Corporation in Cleveland, Ohio, to have a total membership of 90 on the board!

The funding source can also be critical. As an example, the Small Business Administration's 502 program requires that a recipient have at least 25 board members. Several CDCs have expanded their governing boards simply to be eligible for such a loan. The political configuration of the CDC target area can also be important. If a large proportion of the board of directors must be appointed as representatives of community organizations, and there are many such groups, the CDC will find it necessary to maintain a large board.

Selection of the Governing Boards

The mechanisms used to select board members are important since they determine who will be given the official responsibility to act on behalf of the community and the CDC. CDCs have used at least the seven following different mechanisms to select their board members:

1. Self-selection with closed membership. These boards of directors constitute the entire CDC membership and are self-perpetuating, with no formal or legal accountability to any other body, group, or organization.

2. Self-selection with open membership. Such CDCs provide for open membership, but as yet do not have more members than those actually active on their boards of directors.

3. Selection by a community-controlled parent organization. Several CDCs are offshoots of community action agencies or other neighborhood organizations. The parent organization maintains control by appointing a majority of the board members.

4. Selection by a parent other than a community-controlled organization. Churches and other charitable organizations have often sponsored the development of CDCs. Though they may be community-based, they are not community-controlled. They too tend to retain the power to appoint a specified proportion of the CDC board members.

5. Selection from a group of community-based or community-controlled organizations. The organizational form of selection occurs when the CDC membership consists of a coalition of several neighborhood groups. Each member organization appoints or elects a pre-agreed number of board members. This form is sometimes varied in order to bring politically important and/or especially talented individuals onto the CDC board.

6. Selection by membership. Numerous CDCs have memberships in the hundreds of thousands, and selection to the board is by annual elections.

7. Selection by shareholders. Some CDCs have elections to their boards at annual stockholders' meetings. Each person holding stock, no matter how much, has one vote. Community control of elections is maintained by prohibiting the sale or transfer of the stock without CDC approval and by requiring all stockholders leaving the community to sell back to the CDC.[15]

It should be noted that most CDCs use some combination of these mechanisms to select their board members.

Development of the Selection Processes

The choice of the selection mechanism is most strongly influenced by the history of the target area community, by its geographical location, and by the manner in which the CDC was started. To illustrate, the Hough Area Development

Corporation in Cleveland, Ohio, was started largely through the efforts of a minister who was a social-activist organizer. He and a few others selected other community members to participate as board members. They had no ideological or other interest in open elections or even open membership. In 1967, when OEO planners arrived on the scene, they found the board to be reasonably representative of even the radical militants in the Hough community and, impressed by the board's program, they readily accepted its mechanism of self-selection and closed membership. In later years, however, when other CDCs were starting up as the result of planning grants from OEO, "maximum feasible participation," open memberships, and open elections were more strongly pushed. In fact, the Hough CDC has since changed its bylaws to permit open membership to all residents.

Examples of Board Selection Processes

The more typical procedures for board selection can be illustrated by three examples, one each from the nonprofit, for-profit, and cooperative types of CDCs.

Job Start is a nonprofit CDC in southeastern Kentucky that serves about 222,000 people living in ten counties, two-thirds of whom have annual family incomes below $3,000. Its major objective is to create jobs, either by establishing small, wholly owned industries or by investing in larger businesses employing more people. The CDC currently operates three related woodworking and cut-and-sew manufacturaing facilities, all for profit and all under the label of "Possum Trot." From 1970 to 1972 these subsidiaries and Job Start's own offices created 65 jobs in the area. Possum Trot woodworking products and toys are now sold via high-quality mail order catalogs as well as in department stores serving well-to-do customers in major cities. Job Start also invested $250,000 in a corporation, run by a private entrepreneur, that makes tents and other outdoor recreactional products. This produces about 200 more jobs. By 1973 over 400 people were employed through the efforts of Job Start, resulting in an increase in total community income of over $5 million in 1973.

Job Start itself is the parent planning body, controlled by a 14-member board of directors, of which twelve are elected from the existing community action agencies, one of which started Job Start, and other development agencies in the area. Two state-organized area development districts operating within the 10-county area also elect one director each. All of these groups are open to local residents; the bylaws specify that a majority of the directors be poor.

The North Lawndale Economic Development Corporation (NLEDC), which was briefly mentioned in Chapter 2, is a for-profit CDC. It serves an area of Chicago that within 20 years had changed from being all white to 90 percent black. The intention of NLEDC is that community residents will ultimately own and benefit from the CDC's stock, of which there are three classes. Class A voting stock is to be held by community residents, who may purchase up to 20 shares at $5 a share. Class B shares are issued in exchange for capital contributions from OEO (now CSA). These shares are held in an Illinois trust for the benefit of community organizations, particularly NLEDC's parent organization, the Lawndale People's Planning and Action Conference (LPPAC), a nonprofit community group that concentrates on planning for social and economic development. Any profits from NLEDC, apart from the dividends to be paid to resident shareholders, go into this trust. Class C nonvoting stock may be sold to outside residents.

By 1973, NLEDC had received over $10 million from OEO. In addition to its major efforts, which were the construction of a 96-acre industrial park and medical complex in the middle of the ghetto and a 17-acre shopping center (these were also mentioned in Chapter 2), NLEDC is involved in cable television and housing development projects. Land acquisition and relocation of families were major obstacles. Many unemployed and low-skilled residents have been involved in the demolition phases, and more will be involved in the construction phases. Industry is being sought that can train and use the area's low-skilled workers. The medical facility is expected to have a 302-bed nursing center, a group medical practice, a children's center, and a psychiatric hospital.

In 1973 NLEDC had a 21-member board of directors. All were community residents, and 15 were elcted by the shareholders. LPPAC has the legal right to select six of the members. As indicated earlier, this prerogative is commonly included in CDC bylaws for the community organizations that initiate the CDC.

SEASHA, the South East Alabama Self-Help Association, is a cooperative type of CDC serving 12 southeastern Alabama counties, some of which are the most destitute in the nation. Membership is restricted to the residents of the 12 counties; each county elects two board members by secret ballot, and each enterprise is represented by one or two members. The participating residents in each county vote for the board members. Sewer and water facilities are minimal in these counties. About 30 percent of the black families earn less than $1,000 a year, and 40 percent of the entire population, whites as well as blacks, has less than an eighth-grade education. Begun in 1967, SEASHA has assisted 90 locally owned private businesses with loan packaging, management controls, and accounting systems. It has established a credit union for 1,300 people and a 52-family feeder-pig cooperative. SEASHA also helps its members obtain assistance from public social service programs such as aid to dependent children, social security, and so on. It is planning a 300-acre housing and industrial development complex to create more jobs. About 6,500 people currently belong to the cooperative.

Elected versus Appointed Board Members

Neither survey of the CDC boards of directors examined each of the selection processes enumerated above in detail. The Abt survey did inquire, however,

TABLE 3.1

How Membership of the Board Is Determined
(in percent)

	Rural		Urban		Total	
	Chairpersons (N = 11)	Members* (N = 162)	Chairpersons (N = 13)	Members* (N = 178)	Chairpersons (N = 24)	Members (N = 340)
Elected	64	65	39	36	50	50
Appointed	36	35	61	64	50	50
Appointed to represent community organization serving low-income residents	(0)	(14)	(23)	(44)		
Appointed to represent local political group	(0)	(2)	(0)	(0)		
Appointed to represent private sector	(9)	(2)	(8)	(4)		
Appointed to represent business community	(0)	(3)	(8)	(6)		
Appointed to represent public sector	(9)	(2)	(0)	(2)		
Other	(18)	(9)	(23)	(7)		
No answer	(0)	(4)	(0)	(1)		

Note: The no-answer categories were excluded from all statistical tests. The numbers in parentheses indicate the percentage of members appointed by the community interests listed. The total of the numbers in parentheses sum to the percentage for "Appointed" in the table, not to 100.

* p for chi square test < .05.

Source: Author's analysis of the 1972 Abt survey data on CDC board members and chairpersons.

45

whether the board members were elected or appointed and, if appointed, whom they were selected to represent. It also asked whether the board members lived in the CDC target area community. As Table 3.1 shows, approximately one-half of the board chairpersons and board members enter the official CDC leadership by election, the other half by appointment. The location of the CDC is important, however; 64 percent of the urban members but only 35 percent of the rural members are appointed. In addition, while 44 percent of the urban members are appointed to represent community organizations serving low-income residents, only 14 percent of the rural members are. Such data indicate that selection by other community-controlled organizations is much more prevalent in urban than in rural areas. No similar statistically significant differences exist when the boards of directors are compared in terms of the total amount of funds received. In fact, on most variables examined in this chapter no major differences were found when the CDCs are compared in terms of the amounts of funds they had received from OEO. To avoid monotonous repetition of this fact, the results of these analyses will be presented only when they are significant or when the nonsignificance is particularly enlightening.

Place of Residence of Board Members

Almost all CDCs permit nonresidents (persons outside the defined target communities) to have voting memberships. By allowing such "outsiders"

TABLE 3.2

Place of Residence: Board Members and Chairpersons
(in percent)

Place of Residence	Inside CDC Community	Outside CDC Community	No Answer
Rural			
Chairpersons (N = 11)	91	9	—
Members* (N = 162)	96	3	1
Urban			
Chairpersons (N = 13)	69	31	—
Members* (N = 178)	66	33	1
Total			
Chairpersons (N = 24)	79	21	—
Members (N = 340)	80	19	1

* p for chi square test < .05.

Source: Author's analysis of the 1972 Abt survey data on CDC board members and chairpersons.

membership, persons and organizations having businesses and legitimate interests in the target communities, as well as those having skills that supplement those of the "insiders," are brought into the local community economic development acitivity. The data in Table 3.2 show that about 80 percent of all the members of CDC boards of directors are residents of the CDC target area. The appointment mechanism is used to bring outsiders into the organization.

The data in Table 3.2 also show that the rural CDCs have almost all their board members and chairpersons living in the CDC target area communities. The urban CDCs, however, have only about two-thirds of their chairpersons and board members living in the target areas. The reasons for these differences would appear to be that rural areas are more geographically isolated and easier to demarcate—communities do not flow directly into each other as in urban areas—and also that rural areas mix the richer and poorer residents together; people in business, politicians, and other persons of potential influence and experise for the CDC are usually part of the target area. In urban areas the slum consists of many fewer persons of influence and expertise, and therefore appointments from outside to the CDC boards of directors are often needed.

THE DEMOCRATIC NATURE OF THE
SELECTION PROCESSES

Not all CDCs use open elections. Membership in the CDCs has not always been open to all residents, and often access to the CDC is still possible only through other community organizations. These facts raise a basic question about the "community control" aspect of these CDCs. Most Americans tend to equate community control with directly elected representation of the total community. The expectation that open elections are necessarily directly related to democratic control is a strong part of the American ideology. With regard to the CDCs, however, we have found that the members can select themselves into the membership group and/or can be handpicked by a select few previous members and that not everyone in every target areas is automatically eligible to join the official membership of its CDC. We have also found that in selecting the governing boards of the CDCs a significant proportion of the members are appointed rather than elected. How then can such governing boards be considered legitimate representatives of their communities?

To find an adequate answer to this question, it is necessary to examine the comparability of the recruitment of CDC board members with the recruitment procedures of other political and economic bodies. It is also necessary to examine the extent to which such groups use appointment procedures to bring members to their governing boards and to address the general question of how accountable individual governing board members are as a result of having been elected.

Comparability of the Selection Procedures of Community Development Corporations with Those of Business Corporations and City Councils

According to Mace's 1971 study of the selection of directors to large- and medium-sized business corporations in the United States, it is the chief executive officer, the executive director of the operating corporation, who actually chooses who will or will not be on the board of directors.[16] Official nominations and electoral procedures are largely conducted for the sake of form, to satisfy public expectations. For the most part the persons selected to these boards tend to be "chairpersons or presidents of other companies of equal size, top executives of commerical banks, or leading partners of distinguished investment banking and law firms."[17] Variations in the amount of power the chief executive officer has to control the composition of the board of directors occur primarily when one or more shareholders hold a substantial proportion of the company's stock. According to Mace, most of the board members of these business corporations are selected because they have prestigious names and/or titles. Their own high-pressure executive positions almost necessarily preclude their being active, contributing board members.

The description of the selection mechanisms used by the various CDCs should make it clear that the CDC executive officer does not have the same level of dominance in choosing board members as the typical corporation executive. The more established the CDC is, however, the greater the likelihood that the executive director will be able to influence and even determine nominations to the board.

The fact that the CDC itself is a vehicle of community, rather than private, economic development and that consequently the funds used in that development effort are predominantly from governmental sources, almost forces the selection mechanism to be more comparable with the recruitment and selection mechanisms of nonpartisan city councils, that is, political governing boards, than with the mechanisms for selection to the governing boards of economic and business institutions.

In 1970 Kenneth Prewitt reported the results of a 1966-67 study of 435 members of city councils in the greater San Francisco Bay region. All of the cities had nonpartisan councils. Prewitt's study showed that recruitment of candidates for the city councils was strongly related to the past work and interest in the community of the individual and his or her parents, particularly in volunteer work in communitywide activities, knowledge of community problems, acquaintance with other politically active persons, and affiliation with politically active institutions in the community. A diversity of backgrounds, skills, and interests were sought in the members to be elected or appointed to the councils. In contrast to the business corporation, where prestigious names and titles were more necessary prerequisites to nomination to the position of board member than availability to contribute to the board's functioning, the city council selection procedures usually sought persons who were actually willing and able to work on the council, and prestige was a less important factor.[18]

The data in Table 3.3 show that the CDC board members believe they had been selected to their boards primarily for reasons similar to those given by Prewitt for the recruitment of the nonpartisan city council members. The vast majority felt they had been chosen because of their previous involvement in and knowledge of their communities. Relatively few indicated that they felt that they had been chosen because of their previous involvement with community economic development or their business experience, technical skills, or government background. Only one substantial difference was found among the board members in their perceptions of why they had been selected. Compared with the rural members (14 percent), almost double the proportion of urban members (25 percent) felt that they had been selected for their technical skills.

Table 3.3 also reveals that in general the chairpersons are more inclined to think they were chosen for their technical skills, business experience, government backgrounds, or previous work in community economic development than are the regular members. The rural chairpersons differ more from their members than do the urban chairpersons.

In short, CDC board members are not selected for their prestige in the business world; nor are they selected because they are executives of major businesses or corporations. They are selected primarily because of their community and political experience. As will be demonstrated later, there is almost no comparability in the socioeconomic composition of CDC boards with the boards of directors of the large- and medium-sized business corporations studied by Mace, by J. M. Juran and J. Keith Louden, or by Melvin T. Copeland and Andrew R. Towl.[19]

Recruitment to Community Development Corporation and to Political Leadership Roles

It is a truism that in all walks of life and in all community activities, some people lead and others follow. The factual existence of elites that lead and govern is the cornerstone of the social theories of a variety of social philosophers: James Madison, Niccolò Machiavelli, Karl Marx, Gaetano Mosca, Vilfredo Pareto, Plato, and Max Weber, to mention only a few. That the governing bodies in the United States are also elite groups consisting of the tiniest fractions of the total population is evident from the following:

From a national population of nearly 200 million in the United States, several hundred occupy the important government posts at the national level; from a state population of 10 million, about

TABLE 3.3

Self-Perception of Why Selected: Board Members and Chairpersons
(in percent)

	Rural		Urban		Total	
	Chairpersons (N = 11)	Members* (N = 162)	Chairpersons (N = 13)	Members* (N = 178)	Chairpersons (N = 24)	Members (N = 340)
Knowledge of community	73	85	77	82	75	83
Previous community involvement	73	60	77	69	75	65
Previous involvement in community economic development	73	41	54	40	63	40
Business experience	36	30	46	38	42	34
Technical skills	46	14*	39	25*	42	20
Government background	46	12	23	14	33	13

* p for chi square test < .05.
Source: Author's analysis of the 1972 Abt survey data on CDC board members and chairpersons.

180 men hold the important state level elective posts in Ohio; from
a city population of 3.5 million, 50 Chicago aldermen are selected;
from a village population of 7,500, 5 men serve on the Jerseyville
village board. Whatever else government may mean, it certainly
demonstrates that the available political offices number some small
fraction of the population of the community being governed.[20]

In comparison to other governing bodies in the United States, one certainly cannot argue that the CDC governing boards are undemocratic repre-
sentations of their communities on the basis of their small numerical size. In
fact, few people would be concerned with this issue. According to most political scientists, the democratic or nondemocratic nature of the representation
of a community depends not so much on the fraction of the population in the
leadership roles, or even the extent to which power is equally distributed, but
rather on the extent to which all elements have access to power and to the
position of being governing members.[21] It is the recruitment processes that
are at issue, not the selective, elite nature of the governing board that may or
may not result. Kenneth Prewitt describes this reasoning as follows:

In a representative democracy, it is thought to be more important
to control *who* is to gain office than to try and control the behavior
of the incumbent. Theorists, politicans, and citizens alike recognize
that effective, day-to-day control by the people of their governors
is exceedingly difficult. Instead, competitive elections are assumed
to be the mechanism that makes democracy democratic. Men will
compete for office; the voters will choose; and democratic government will be assured.[22]

Prewitt's study of the recruitment of citizen-politicians to the nonpartisan city councils in the San Francisco Bay Area revealed that long before any
of the city council members had even had their names presented to their communities for election, the recruitment processes had begun. To illustrate, the
social bias in leadership selection effectively eliminated the less educated and
poorer 60 percent of the community! Interestingly enough, it also eliminated
the majority of the better-educated and most wealthy citizens. The physiological
characteristics of parts of the population also effectively eliminated many
potential candidates: being female eliminated almost 50 percent of the eligible
population. Certain racial, ethnic, and religious backgrounds precluded others.
Hence, the existing cultural norms and the societal expectations about the
characteristics that leaders and politically active people should have effectively
reduces the proportion of the population who have the option of even selecting
themselves into the recruitment process, much less of being selected as a part
of the governing few.

Becoming a member of a community development corporation is not
unlike becoming part of the politically and economically active stratum of a

community. In each case the individual's family background, personal acquaintances, previous education and occupational experiences, beliefs and dispositions about the world, and physiological characteristics set the framework for whether or not that person will, first, know about the CDC's existence; second, be inclined to join; and third, actually select himself or herself into the community economic development movement.

This process and result are similar to those observed by Prewitt in the 87 cities he studied. On the basis of the Bay Area findings he concluded:

> By this criterion [having equal access to the values on which political recruitment is based], municipal government in the Bay Area is not egalitarian. The uneven distribution of the antecedent roles, the traits, and skills, the self-images and aspirations, the contacts, the knowledge and experiences, and the class attributes which further political careers result in the uneven contribution of different social strata to political leadership.[23]

Although it is certainly true that any CDC whose constitution restricts membership is undemocratic, the CDCs with open memberships cannot be faulted simply because a majority of the residents have chosen not to select themselves or allow themselves to be co-opted into their community's politically and economically active stratum. The process of choosing those who will lead a population in specific activities begins with the process of eliminating, usually by self-selection, the vast majority of the population that is to be represented and governed. This is part of representative democracy. The fact that the CDC is a cross between a private and a public institution makes it less likely that a majority of its residents will ever become official members.

It appears, however, that the more successful the CDC is in producing economic change, the more probable it is that large community memberships will result. Howard W. Hallman notes that participation in elections for community corporation boards has steadily increased in New York with an increase in the corporation's visibility in the community. He also reports that "elsewhere, when the neighborhood body has substantive power, turnout is greater—amounting to 25 percent in some model cities' elections, a figure which compares with nonpartisan elections for city councilmen and school board members in many communities."[24] A central problem in assessing the democratic nature of CDCs, however, is the fact that often organizations, rather than persons, are defined as the potential members. The liberal democratic tradition rests upon the assumption that individuals, not groups or associations, are the basic participating units in society.

Use of the Appointment Mechanism in Community Development Corporations and in Nonpartisan City Councils

Two-thirds of all the urban CDC governing board members and one-third of the rural CDC governing board members are appointed to their offices. This raises an important question about the extent to which they and the board as a whole can be considered accountable to the community. Again, in responding to this issue, a political perspective is helpful. In his study Prewitt found that a full 25 percent of the city council members in the 87 Bay Area cities had initially been appointed, not elected, to their offices.[25] While the percentage of CDC appointments is higher, particularly in the urban areas, the fact remains that appointment to a political governing board, like appointment to the board of a business institution, is a common procedure. The reasons for using appointments are also generally similar. An appointment can insure a like-minded successor, can help to develop or maintain a working coalition on the governing board, and can co-opt hostile or potentially hostile elements of the community into the governing group.

Logically, it would seem that at least the rural CDC governing boards cannot be considered unrepresentative of the communities they serve simply on the grounds of appointment of their boards of directors unless the 87 Bay Area city councils are also to be considered unrepresentative on the same grounds. In rural areas the appointment percentage is only slightly higher for the CDCs than it is for the Bay Area councils.

In urban areas the proportion of appointed board members is almost two-thirds of the entire governing board. This appointment level is clearly out of line with what seems to be acceptable practice for political governing boards. We must ask: Why did this situation develop in urban areas? Can such governing boards, constituted by the appointment rather than by the elective mechanism, be seriously considered legitimate representatives of their communities? The answers to both questions are intimately related to whether or not and how community representatives can be held accountable.

Probably more than any other agency of the federal government, OEO long sought to use the elective process as a means of bringing the poor, and their target area communities, into the decision-making process and onto governing boards. OEO planners seemed to think that if they could get boards that were socioeconomically representative of their constituencies, then greater accountability to that constituency would result. After much turmoil and strife and many program failures, OEO learned that in urban areas in particular this theory was simply not true: Americans pay lip service to participation in local elections more than they actually participate. Research continually demonstrates that "the most important feature of participation in community politics is how little there is of it."[26] One study of local elections in 676 U.S. cities in a nonpresidential election year found that less than one-third of the potential electorate actually voted in citywide elections.[27] The national fact of life for all Americans, not just the poor, "and it overshadows almost everything else, is that *most citizens use their political resources scarcely at all.*"[28]

That the electorate in poor communities does not vote in neighborhood elections should, therefore, not be too surprising. The lower educational levels, the lack of familiarity with registration requirements, the lack of clarity of issues, the high proportion of new migrants, and the general disillusionment with the efficacy of the electoral process in delivering positive ends for the poor all contribute to a lower level of participation. At best the Community Action Agencies and the Model City elections have turned out a vote of 10 percent. The average turnout has usually been closer to 5 percent.[29] These low turnouts of voters rapidly turned off many early advocates of maximum feasible participation who had particularly emphasized participation through the election process. Daniel Moynihan wrote about this as follows:

> The devise [sic] of holding elections among the poor to choose representatives for the CAP governing boards made the program look absurd. The turnouts in effect declared that the poor weren't interested: in Philadelphia 2.7 percent; Los Angeles 0.7 percent; Boston 2.4 percent; Cleveland 4.2 percent; Kansas City, M. 5.0 percent. Smaller communities sometimes got larger turnouts, but never anything nearly approaching that of a listless off-year election.[30]

Because the poor were not voting, the governing boards could easily be railroaded. Even if they weren't, they could easily be dominated by strong personalities or strong interest groups. Corruption, distortion of goals, misuse of funds, and other problems were as often promoted as prohibited by such elections. Under these circumstances it is not surprising that a large number of urban CDCs have chosen the organizational form of selection over the open-election mechanism. It also would not be surprising if "community control" were greater in these areas, where board members are accountable to community organizations rather than to an amorphous electorate.

Another problem was that a community defined on the basis of its negative characteristics and made into an electoral district seldom constitutes a psychological community capable of acting as a concerned, responsive constituency. Even if an elected representative wanted to report to someone, there often was no organized body representing the electorate to whom he or she could report. The elected board members in many early community action programs found themselves so isolated and feeling so separated from their constituencies that many did not even feel an obligation to attend meetings. Ralph M. Kramer reports that eight months after an election in one California city, only one out of the eight elected representatives even bothered going to board meetings.[31] Over the years both accountability to the community and representation of the interests of the poor community as a whole have increased, in the view of many black activists, by eliminating the communitywide election requirement. In its place the appointment mechanism is used; neighborhoods or other communitywide organizations, such as a CAP agency, select board members, and then each group regularly receives a report on the progress of both the board member and the project.

The Problem of Organizational Representation

Those in favor of organizational representation and the use of the appointment mechanism rather than open elections argue that organizational representation most effectively fulfills the chief functions of representation: "(a) to satisfy specific articulate demands and (b) to co-opt the agitators who have rendered these demands important political issues."[32] Alan A. Altshuler notes that organizations are essential mobilization mechanisms in their communities. Individuals need linkages to established structures if either community or economic progress is to take place.[33] As Sar Levitan pointed out, unless individuals run on political parties or organizational platforms that incorporate known symbols into the election process, residents have no ready way of relating issues, proposal programs, and objectives to their experience—past, present, or future.[34] Defenders of organizational representation on the CDC governing boards also stress that the organizations permitted to appoint members to the CDC boards of directors usually themselves have open membership for all neighborhood residents and use elections to fill their main offices. Hence organizational representation is simply indirect representation.

The opponents of organizational representation argue that it will become increasingly less representative of the population over time. The initial "charter members" will write the bylaws in such a way that their own seats are secure, making it harder for the governing board to be truly representative even of the organizations in the community.[35] In fact, a few CDCs have done this. For example, the Harlem Commonwealth Council has a board of directors consisting of 30 members. Of these, 12 seats are reserved for the original founders or for their internally elected replacements. Another 10 members are representative of other community organizations operating in Harlem, such as local branches of the NAACP and the Urban League and church groups. The remaining 8 members are elected by the United Block Association, a neighborhood-based coalition of Harlem residents.[36] Such boards seem to be heading toward informal establishment of an "upper house" that is to be uneffected by the whims and wishes of the masses and a "lower house" elected to reflect the views of residents and community organizations. So far, however, there has been no real attempt to separate the different groups on CDC boards into coequal deliberative bodies. The small number of members probably precludes this development. Whether or not this CDC board will become decreasingly representative of the Harlem community is a question that can be answered only by empirical study of that community and its CDC over a period of time.

Other arguments against organizational representation include (1) the possibility that special interest groups within organizations represented on the board, or the whole organization itself, could intimidate governing board members to act counter to the interest of the whole community; (2) the fact that representatives from organizations with extremist views tend to disrupt the CDC activities, leading to possible conflict with funding sources; and (3) the very real concern that funding sources, particularly governmental agencies, will maintain that the CDC governing board is not representative because the selection procedures are not based on open elections.[37] In terms of what has actually happened to CDCs, the first problem of special interest groups is a real one that does need guarding against.[38] The second problem has not been serious for any CDC that I know of. The third problem is usually avoided by requiring that the organizations that are eligible for membership in the CDC themselves have open access for all residents of the categories they serve.

Choosing a Selection Process to Produce Greatest Representation and Accountability

Although the arguments against organizational representation and selection of CDC board members by the appointment mechanism are persuasive, the arguments against relying upon the election process alone are also persuasive. Both OEO's experience and the research on nonpartisan city councils tend to support the view that accountability is *not* assured by elections alone.

Most theorists still argue that elected officials are held accountable and operate within limits because of "their expectations about what policies they can adopt and still be reelected."[39] As Prewitt points out, however, this supposed guarantee of the accountability of the elected official assumes two things: (1) that the official has in fact been elected, not appointed, to fill a vacancy and (2) that the people holding governing board positions actually want to keep them and therefore respond to the wishes of the electorate.[40] In his study of the 87 Bay Area city councils, these assumptions did not hold. A full one-fourth of the supposedly elected officials had been appointed. In addition, few officials who had stood for reelection had been defeated. About 80 percent of the incumbents had been reelected. In 21 cities all of the incumbents had been reelected. Moreover, over half of the city council members had set a self-imposed limit on the time they would serve; that is, they were voluntarily determining when they would retire. According to Prewitt, almost none of them were even concerned about the voting of the electorate in developing their retirement plans. He concludes, "The findings indicate that the student of politics who would base his theory of representative democracy on the power of elections to enforce accountability would be making untenable assumptions about the Bay Area cities."[41]

Time has been spent on the Bay Area city council study for two reasons. First, the citizen-politicians on these nonpartisan city councils hold positions in their citywide communities that are generally similar to, but even more public, than those held by the CDC board members in their neighborhood communities. The city council data provide a point of comparison for the CDC board member data, making conclusions about the latter data more meaningful and valid.

Second, the issue of community control is controversial. Both OEO and its programs have been severely criticized for their failure to achieve high voter turnout in their elections and for the results of the elections that did not produce accountable elected officials. The Bay Area city council study demonstrates that it is not reasonable to assume that elections will necessarily produce such accountability.

The comparison also raises an important question about what criteria should be used to determine whether appropriate community control mechanisms actually exist. The American political ideology and many political theorists argue, "Just look to see if an election has been held with community-wide suffrage." Empirical reality, however, indicates that such a simple requirement is insufficient. Whatever final criteria are chosen, we must be careful not to apply a double standard. The mechanisms for producing community control and accountability in poor neighborhoods should not be determined by the myths of ideology while the mechanisms for producing accountability in citywide areas are determined by what actually works.

Unfortunately, at the end of this discourse on the process by which board members are selected, it is still not possible to conclude definitely that the CDC governing boards are accountable to and appropriately representative of their communities. The typical liberal preference for open elections is partly based on the view that it is this process itself that makes a system democratic. If the people freely choose governing boards from some existing elite group, then no one should complain or interfere. The people, it is argued, could have chosen people just like themselves if they so wanted. When elections produce reasonably large turnouts, such a conclusion might be justified, but how can this argument hold if only 5 percent of the people vote? Must the 5 percent who do vote be representative of their neighborhood communities in a systematic, probability-sample sense? At the moment we can conclude only that CDC governing boards are accountable at least to those who choose to vote and to the organizations they represent. Whether that is sufficient is a judgmental question, to which individuals' answers will depend on their prior experience in low-income environments, their emotional and philosophical attachment to the election process itself, and the way they evaluate the outcome of the various selection procedures in terms of the characteristics of the board members selected.[42] In September 1975, CSA issued an instruction on composition and selection of CDC boards of directors that was fairly flexible and granted some leeway, based on local needs and conditions and on size, residency, representation requirements, and selection procedures.

THE RESULTING REPRESENTATIVENESS
OF THE BOARD MEMBERS

Background Characteristics

One of the ways in which people try to determine whether a governing group is "representative" of those governed is to see whether the selection procedures result in a body of officials who are comparable with those being governed—if they have a similarity of view point or socioeconomic background. To what extent can CDC governing boards be considered "legitimate" representatives of their communities in terms of their background characteristics? Since data on the comparability of the board members' and residents' views on specific issues are not currently available, that type of representativeness cannot be addressed.

From the presentation so far, it should be clear that CDC boards of directors are not likely to be the run-of-the-mill poverty people of the stereotypes. The background data demonstrate this fact.

Sex. Like most economic and business organizations in the United States, the CDC boards of directors are almost entirely male. Only 21 percent of all the members surveyed by Abt in July 1972 were women. One (4 percent) of the total 24 chairpersons was a woman. The Kelly survey in the fall of 1973 found that, for all the CDCs, only 26 percent of the board members were women. (See Table 3.4.) The urban CDCs had a higher proportion of women (30 percent) than the rural CDCs (20 percent), but this difference is not statistically significant. In 1973 not even one chairperson was a woman.

TABLE 3.4

Sex of Board Members and Chairpersons, 1973
(in percent)

	Female	Male	No Answer
Members			
Rural (N = 108)	20	79	1
Urban (N = 165)	30	70	0
Total			
Chairpersons (N = 19)	0	100	0
Members (N = 273)	26	73	1
Members of corporations of			
Less than $2 million (N = 193)	27	73	0
$2 million or more (N = 80)	24	73	3

Source: The author's 1973 survey of CDC board members and chairpersons.

TABLE 3.5

Racial Background of Board Members, 1972
(in percent)

	Rural* (N = 162)	Urban* (N = 178)	Total (N = 340)
Black	41	78	61
Indian	10	0	5
White	44	13	28
Other	0	2	1
No answer	4	6	5

* p for chi square test < .05.

Source: Author's analysis of 1972 Abt survey data on CDC board members and chairpersons.

Race. The variable of race inevitably produces statistically significant results when used in analyzing OEO programs, political power, or economic organizations. Here the variations in race reflect the nature and history not only of poverty in the United States but also of OEO program support for CDCs. The OEO program was originally designed as a response to the 1969 final report of the National Commission on the Causes and Prevention of Violence, which had brought attention to the need for more business development and self-determination in black urban ghettos. To get support for the enabling legislation from rural members of Congress, however, OEO had to agree to apply the program to rural areas with high outmigration rates. Since in rural areas the white poor outnumber the black poor, it was inevitable that eventually they would get at least equal attention from OEO. As Tables 3.5 and 3.6 show, the proportion of white and nonwhite board members in the CDC program did not change between 1972 and 1973. About 28 percent of the board members were white and about two-thirds were nonwhite. Both tables also show that the board members in urban areas tend to predominantly black (78 percent in the 1972 survey and 52 percent in the 1973 survey). In rural areas the proportions of black and white members are closer; in 1972 the proportion each was almost the same, 41 percent for blacks and 44 percent for whites. (See Table 3.5.)

The results from the Kelly survey in 1973 are quite similar, but because of the way the question was asked, they are more specific. In the 1973 question the nonwhites were able to choose Mexican-American and Puerto Rican designations as well as black and Indian. While almost the same percentage of whites are board members, the proportion of blacks is reduced, approximately by the amount of responses of Mexican-Americans and Puerto Ricans. (See Table 3.6.)

TABLE 3.6

Racial Background of Board Members, 1973
(in percent)

	Rural* (N = 108)	Urban* (N = 165)	Total (N = 273)
Black	32	52	44
Indian	8	1	4
Mexican-American	16	13	14
Puerto Rican	0	4	2
White	42	18	27
No answer	2	13	8

* p for chi square test < .05.
Source: The author's 1973 survey of CDC board members.

It should be noted, however, that part of the variation found here between 1972 and 1973 data on the proportion of blacks is due to the fact that different CDCs were included in the two samples. The 1972 survey included more of the CDCs that were funded earliest by OEO, which tended to be primarily in black ghetto areas. The 1973 survey included a higher proportion of the more recently funded CDCs (1970 and later); Spanish-speaking minorities had been included in these CDCs to a much greater extent than they had been in the CDCs funded earlier.[43] (See Chapter 1 for a discussion of the difference in sample frames between the two surveys.)

The comparison on the basis of the total amounts of funds received from OEO up to fiscal 1974 further reflects the history of the OEO program. The largest proportion of the board members of all CDCs, regardless of funding level, is black; but in the 1972 Abt survey, 69 percent of the board members of CDCs having received $2 million or more were black, while 54 percent of those having received less than $2 million were not. The largest CDCs in terms of OEO funds also tend to be those that were funded in fiscal 1969 or earlier, precisely in those years when the OEO emphasis was still almost solely on black urban ghettos. If the CDC program continues to survivie, it would seem to be only a matter of time before this direct relationship between funding level and race will disappear. This is not to say that whites will receive an increasingly large share of all funds, but rather that those CDCs consisting of more white members will, as they continue their development, follow a path of growth somewhat similar to that of the other CDCs. Over a ten-year period the total amount and rate of funding should not differ significantly for the predominantly black or predominantly white CDCs. Although there are more white poor people than black poor people, there is little possibility that white CDCs will someday dominate the program. The decline of the "war on poverty" and the current lack of federal funds and publicity for the CDC program reduces to zero the chance that this change will take place in the near future.

The 1972 Abt survey of the racial backgrounds of the board chairpersons revealed that, relatively speaking, more whites were chairpersons in 1972 than would be anticipated on the basis of the percentages of blacks and whites on the boards of directors in general. While 28 percent of all board members were white, 42 percent of all board chairpersons were. (See Table 3.7; compare with Table 3.5.) Further, 64 percent of the rural chairpersons were white, but only 44 percent of the rural members were. Among the urban CDCs this difference is less pronounced; 13 percent of the members and 23 percent of the chairpersons were white. The comparison of funding levels using the $2 million split shows a similar pattern: 19 percent of the members of the wealthier CDCs were white, but 33 percent of the chairpersons were. Among the less-funded CDCs, 36 percent of the members and 50 percent of the chairpersons were white.

The 1973 Kelly survey found no such sharp differences among the chairpersons and members in terms of racial-ethnic background. In that survey 21 percent of the chairpersons were white (see Table 3.8), and 27 percent of the members surveyed were white (see Table 3.6). As the data in Chapter 4 will show, the 1973 data, as well as the 1972 data, support the conclusion that the chairpersons are selected by the members on the basis of experience, education, knowledge, and length of time as board members. Racial-ethnic background does not seem to be a constant factor in the choice, although in any one year racial and ethnic imbalances may occur.

TABLE 3.7

Racial Background of Chairpersons, 1972
(in percent)

	Rural* (N = 11)	Urban* (N = 13)	Total (N = 24)	In Corporations of	
				Less than $2 million (N = 12)	$2 million or more (N = 12)
Black	27	69	50	50	50
Indian	9	0	4	0	8
White	64	23	42	50	33
Other	0	8	4	0	8

* p for Fisher extract one-tailed test < .13.
Source: Author's analysis of 1973 Abt survey data on CDC chairpersons.

TABLE 3.8

Racial Background of Chairpersons, 1973
(in percent)

	Nonwhite	White
Rural (N = 9)	67	33
Urban (N = 10)	90	10
Total (N = 19)	79	21
In corporations of		
Less than $2 million (N = 13)	77	23
$2 million or more (N = 6)	83	17

Source: The author's 1973 survey of CDC chairpersons.

Age. The data from both the 1972 Abt survey and the 1973 Kelly survey reveal similar trends in the age patterns of the board members. In both years the largest percentage of board members fell in the 35-49 age group (41 percent in 1972 and 39 percent in 1973). The 50-plus age group had the next-largest percentage represented (about 30 percent in 1972 and 36 percent in 1973). Roughly 22 percent of the members were 34 years old or younger, in 1973, 17 percent were. The age distributions of the board members did not vary significantly by funding level in either sample, but again, the rural-urban comparisons did, reflecting to a large extent the age distributions of the populations served by the CDCs. In both surveys the urban board members tended to be younger on the average than the rural members.

The age distributions of the chairpersons for the 1972 data appear to reflect not so much the population curves of the areas, but rather the ages at which effective leadership is at a premium. In 1972 the urban CDCs tended to select members who were 50 or older as their chairpersons, which is interesting given the relative scarcity of black business leaders in this age category. Rural CDCs tended to choose as their chairpersons individuals between 35 and 49. The 1973 data reveal that, overall, the 34-49 age group is the most prevalent among the chairpersons.

Education. The most notable difference between the board members and their chairpersons was their educational attainment. While 42 percent of the members in 1972 had a high school diploma or less, only 21 percent of the chairpersons had. Conversely, while 79 percent of the chairpersons had had some college training or a college degree and/or advanced college work, only 58 percent of the members had. In 1972 the severest educational gap between chairpersons and members occurred in the rural areas, where 64 percent of the chairpersons had some graduate work, a master's degree, or a Ph.D., while only 12 percent of the members had. Indeed, 39 percent of the members did not have high school diplomas. The urban board members had significantly more formal education than their rural counterparts.

Area of Academic Specialization. The data on area of academic specilization showed no major differences between rural and urban members. About half the members of each group had chosen business or economics when they went to college. The members of the less-funded CDCs majored in business and/or economics significantly more often than the members of the better-funded CDCs.

Whether academic specialization in business and economics is helpful in efforts at community economic development is still open to question. It may not be. The academic training is usually in a Keynesian or classical economic tradition, which is not entirely compatible with the community economic development effort.[44] It is possible that such training produces static that needs to be counteracted. Economists, like the members of most other social science disciplines, have a reluctance, which Galbraith has so well described, to accommodate underlying change. The consequence of this reluctance, he notes, "is that, in time of social and institutional change, the advice on practical matters which reflects the accepted economic view will often and perhaps usually be in error. The advice will relate to previous and not to present institutions."[45]

Occupational-Economic Position of Community Development Corporation Leaders

Types of Institutions by which They Are Employed.

In 1972 about two-thirds of the board members (66 percent) and slightly more than one-half of the chairpersons (54 percent) worked in institutions concerned essentially with business or economic development. (See Table 3.9.) Sharp differences in the types of institution the board members work for do not exist, whether the $2 million split or the rural-urban comparison is used, or the chairpersons are compared to the members.

The critical difference is the proportion of self-employed members versus the employed proportion. While 44 percent of the rural members were self-employed, 25 percent of the urban members were not. Similarly, while 38 percent of the members of CDCs receiving less than $2 million were self-employed, 29 percent of the members of CDCs receiving $2 million or more were not.

The sharpest difference found in the data on the type of institution that employed the members was that between the rural and urban chairpersons. Of the rural chairpersons, 100 percent were either self-employed (18 percent) or employed by a university or school (36 percent), bank/lending institution (9 percent), local business development group (9 percent), or community

TABLE 3.9

Types of Institutions Employing Board Members and Chairpersons
(in percent)

Institutions	Chairpersons (N = 24)	Members (N = 340)
Business-economic	54	66
Bank or lending institution	(4)	(3)
Local business	(21)	(17)
Industry	(8)	(8)
Local business development group	(8)	(4)
Self-employed	(13)	(34)
Other	46	34
University or school	(25)	(9)
Church	(4)	(3)
Local political body	(0)	(1)
Community agency	(13)	(13)
Government agency	(4)	(8)

Note: The numbers in parentheses indicate the percentages of the total employed by specific types of institutions under the two major categories—business-economic and other.

Source: Author's analysis of 1972 Abt survey data on CDC chairpersons and board members.

agency (27 percent). In contrast, only 38 percent of the urban chairpersons were not self-employed. The urban chairpersons were generally employed by a local business (39 percent); the remainder were employed by industry (15 percent), a university or school (15 percent), a local business development group (8 percent), a government agency (8 percent), a church (7 percent), or self-employed (7 percent).

Type of Position

The bulk of the CDC board members indicated that they had fairly high-level positions within the institutions that employed them. Forty-seven percent said they were managers or proprietors of their institutions; 15 percent said they were professionals working with people, and 3 percent said they were professionals dealing with data. Only 18 percent indicated that they were working in sales, in clerical positions, as skilled or semiskilled workers, in domestic or other services, or as nonfarm laborers. Another 18 percent said they were farm workers. Significant differences exist among the members in terms of the amounts of money their CDCs had received from OEO and between those in

TABLE 3.10

Types of Occupational Positions Held by Board Members
(in percent)

	Rural* (N = 162)	Urban* (N = 178)	Total (N = 340)	In Corporations of	
				Less than $2 million (N = 184)	$2 million or More* (N = 156)
Professional	17	20	18	14	23
Managers	37	56	47	51	42
Sales, clerical, skilled laborers	8	6	8	5	10
Unskilled, nonfarm laborers	14	7	10	12	8
Farm laborer	24	12	18	18	17

* p for chi square test < .05.
Source: Author's analysis of 1972 Abt survey data on CDC board members.

rural and those in urban CDCs. Only 54 percent of the rural board members indicated that they had professional or managerial positions, but 76 percent of the urban members did. (See Table 3.10.) Prior to fiscal 1974, the CDCs that had received $2 million or more from OEO had fewer unskilled laborers, fewer managers and proprietors, and more professionals and skilled laborers than the CDCs that had received less than $2 million.

Almost all of the board chairpersons were professionals, managers, or proprietors (84 percent). Of those who were not, two classified themselves as farm workers, one as a skilled worker, and the other as a service worker.

Monthly Salary. As was indicated earlier, the CDC governing boards are located in low-income areas and are supposed to represent such areas. If we use the criterion of low income, as OEO occasionally has, then we cannot say that the CDC board members are representative of their communities. Only 21 percent of those who responded indicated that they earned $500 or less per month. (See Table 3.11.) That is the equivalent of $6,000 per year, which is considerably above the 1972-73 OEO poverty guidelines for both rural and urban areas. Another 20 percent said they earned between $501 and $900 per month (between $6,000 and $10,800 per year); another 17 percent stated that they earned $901-$1,300 a month (between $10,800 and $15,600 a year); and another 11 percent indicated that they earned more than $15,000 a year. On the average, the chairpersons tended to earn more than the board members. While 42 percent said they earned more than $900 a month, only 28 percent of the members said they earned that much. As one would expect, the urban members earn much more than the rural ones. The rural chairpersons, however, earn the most money. Given their educational levels, which are considerably greater than those of their urban counterparts, one would expect this greater earning power.

Prior Work Experience

In an effort to get a general picture of the past work experience the board members bring to bear on the problems of community economic development, the respondents in the Kelly survey were asked to indicate whether they had work experience with the 11 different types of institutions listed in Table 3.12. They were also asked to indicate whether they had worked in managerial or professional positions, as board members, advisors, or trustees, and whether that experience was helping them in their jobs as CDC board members.

The results in Table 3.12 show that even though about one-half of the board members have had experience in local businesses, relatively few, whether rural or urban, have had experience in banks and lending institutions, industry, union, or business development groups (about one-fourth in each category). The proportion of all the board members having held managerial or professional

TABLE 3.11

Monthly Salaries of Board Members and Chairpersons, 1972
(in percent)

| | Geographical Location | | | | | | Total OEO Funding of Corporation of | | | |
| | Rural | | Urban | | Total | | Less than $2 Million | | $2 million or More | |
Salary Level	Chairpersons (N = 11)	Members* (N = 162)	Chairpersons (N = 13)	Members* (N = 178)	Chairpersons (N = 24)	Members (N = 340)	Chairpersons (N = 12)	Members* (N = 184)	Chairpersons (N = 12)	Members* (N = 156)
$500 or less	0	35	15	8	8	21	17	23	0	18
$501-900	9	20	23	19	17	20	8	15	25	25
$901-1,300	36	9	23	24	29	17	42	20	17	13
$1,301 plus	18	4	8	17	13	11	25	15	0	6
No answer	37	32	31	32	33	31	8	27	58	38

* p for chi square test < .05.
Source: Author's analysis of 1972 Abt survey data on CDC board members and chairpersons.

positions in these types of institutions hovered around 10 percent of the entire sample of 273. The proportion of members who had been or then were board members, advisors, or trustees of such institutions is similarly low, although about 18 percent of both the rural and the urban members said they either had been or were board members of other business development groups in their areas as well as being CDC board members.

The experience that the majority of urban CDC board members bring to their task is work with neighborhood associations (64 percent), churches (58 percent), community agencies (52 percent), and local political bodies (51 percent). The rural members also have a majority who have had work experience with churches (62 percent) and community agencies (54 percent), but unlike those in the urban CDCs, only 46 percent were experienced in neighborhood associations and, perhaps more importantly, 56 percent had experience in local business, whereas a smaller 43 percent of the urban members did. About two-fifths of all the board members had had some work experience in schools or universities, and two-fifths had worked in government agencies. No significant variations in the work experience of board members was found by the amount of funds their respective CDCs had received from OEO.

Participation in the Economic, Social, and Decision-Making Life of Communities

Just as community wide suffrage is a part of America's ideological heritage, so also is the view that Americans, particularly middle- and upper-class Americans, are joiners, members of many organizations. This popular stereotype is not quite true, however, as several political scientists have noted. Warner Bloomberg, Jr., and Florence W. Rosenstock describe the actual state of participation as follows:

> The majority of American citizens belong to only one or two organizations, if any, and for the most part are passive members rather than part of the active core of any associations to which they belong. Moreover, only a small proportion of those associations are normally relevant to or in any way affect the kind of decision making with which "maximum feasible participation" is concerned; usually they serve other individual and institutional goals, most often those having to do with religion, job security, and recreation and sociability. And when acutal involvement in roles most directly concerned with making community decisions apart from elections is examined, the proportions drop below the 10 percent level.[46]

Against this backdrop of what is typical for most Americans everywhere, the CDC board members are indeed exceptionally active in their communities.

One might expect the board chairpersons, because of their position of leadership, to be more involved in community affairs than their member

TABLE 3.12

Prior Work Experience of Board Members, by Rural-Urban Comparison
(in percent)

	Worked with Groups Listed		Held in Managerial or Professional Position		Functioned as a Board Member, Advisor or Trustee		Found that this Experience Helped CDC Board Member*	
	Rural (N = 108)	Urban (N = 165)	Rural (N = 108)	Urban (N = 165)	Rural (N = 108)	Urban (N = 165)	Rural	Urban
Banking or lending institution	19	18	6	12	12	9	74	83
School university	40	40	23	22	12	13	80	83
Local business	56*	43 *	32	32	24	14	79	81
Industry	23	29	12	18	10	6	83	72
Church	62	58	17	17	39	31	79	66
Business development group Chamber of Commerce	30	23	7	7	18	17	70	83
Neighborhood association (such as a local coop or a gang)	46	64	17	21	26	43	76	89
Local political body (such as a local citizen association)	47	51	19	17	26	35	68	86
Community agency (such as community action programs)	54	52	15	20	32	38	76	92
Government agency (Federal, state, or local)	32	41	19	26	14	16	75	80
Union	19	27	7	9	8	12	68	70

*The N for each percentage here is based upon the number who indicated they had worked with groups listed. For example, the 83 under "Urban" should be read as follows: 83 percent of the 18 percent who said they worked with banking and lending institutions said this experience helped them as CDC board members.

Source: The author's 1973 survey of CDC board members.

TABLE 3.13

Participation of Board Members in Economic, Social, and Decision-making Life of Community
(in percent)

| | Rural | | Urban | | Total | | Total OEO Funding | | | |
| | | | | | | | Less than $2 Million | | $2 Million or More | |
	Chairpersons (N = 11)	Members (N = 162)	Chairpersons (N = 13)	Members (N = 178)	Chairpersons (N = 24)	Members (N = 340)	Chairpersons (N = 12)	Members (N = 184)	Chairpersons (N = 12)	Members (N =156)
Belong to economic and/or local business development groups										
Yes	46	29*	54	43*	50	36	33	38	67	35
No	55	67*	46	57*	50	61	67	60	33	63
No response	0	4	0	1	0	2	0	3	0	1
Number of offices held										
No response	64	86	69	77	67	81	83	83	50	79
1	18	11	31	21	25	16	8	14	42	19
2 or more	18	3	0	2	8	3	8	3	8	2
Belong to community groups, social clubs, or organizations										
Yes	45	71*	54	84*	50	77	50	77	50	78
No	27	28*	15	16*	21	22	17	22	25	21
No response	27	1	31	0	29	1	33	1	25	1
Number of offices held										
No response	82	51	62	50	71	50	75	53	67	47
1	18	30	15	32	17	31	17	30	17	32
2 or more	0	19	23	19	13	19	8	17	17	21
Member of decision-making bodies in community										
Yes	38	34	11	29	17	31	25	34	8	28
No	63	63	89	70	54	66	42	55	67	70
No response	0	3	0	1	28	2	33	11	25	1

* p for chi square text < .05.
Source: Author's analysis of 1972 Abt survey data on CDC board members and chairpersons.

counterparts; but this does not seem to be true. Rather, it appears that variation in extent of participation between the chairpersons and members depends upon the type of organization. For example, a higher percentage of board chairpersons than members (50 percent to 36 percent) belong to economic and local business development groups, and about one-third of the chairpersons hold an office in such organizations, while only about one-fifth of the members do. (See Table 3.13.) The statistics are quite different, however, for membership in community and social groups. Here a larger percentage of board members are involved than board chairpersons (77 percent compared to 50 percent). About one-half of the chairpersons (17 percent), compared to the members (31 percent), participate in decision-making bodies in the community. (See Table 3.13.)

The comparison of the board members by geographical location shows that the urban members, significantly more often than the rural members, belong to economic or local business development groups and to community groups, social clubs, and organizations. The proportion belonging to community and social groups is about double or more for both urban and rural members as that belonging to economic and business groups. In terms of membership in overall decision-making bodies in the community, however, no sharp difference between the rural and the urban members appears.

The chairpersons do not vary significantly in their participation patterns at all.

CONCLUSION

This chapter began with these questions: What is the "community" in community economic development? Who represents this community and controls the community development corporations formed to implement the community economic development program? To what extent can these governing boards be considered legitimate representatives of their communities?

The answer to the first question was found to depend upon the geographical location of the CDC, but in general it applies to low-income areas, either within specified neighborhoods of large cities or several counties in rural areas. The definition of a representative of a community to be served was found to be different from the definition of eligibility to become a member of a CDC, since CDCs do not automatically include all residents as members. Because residents must select themselves into the CDC membership, CDC memberships and boards of directors tend to come from among the more active community residents and from the socioeconomically better-off elements of these low-income communities.

As a general rule, throughout the United States the socioeconomic and participatory characteristics of official and de facto leaders are not typical of those governed or led. Invariably the leaders come from the active higher socioeconomic groups of their communities. The variations in socioeconomic representation are important, however, in the extent to which the governing individuals deviate from the characteristics of the general population. Recent studies seem to indicate that the characteristics of the selected leadership will be directly and systematically affected by the socioeconomic characteristics of the communities from which the leaders are selected.[47] Hence, while a social class disparity usually exists between leaders and followers, within most U.S. communities the disparity is kept within relatively reasonable bounds. The CDC boards fall into this national pattern. The members of the CDC governing boards tend to be the opinion leaders of their poverty areas. The boards are mainly middle class in composition, and they represent a much higher proportion of business and economic interests than is usual for groups in such areas. Over one-half of the 1973 sample and close to two-thirds of the 1972 sample of CDC board members have business, banking, industrial, and other economic types of work backgrounds. Nonetheless, these boards are still more similar to a community action program board of directors and to nonpartisan city councils than to the boards of directors of the citywide banks serving the CDC areas.

The data indicate that while the CDC boards of directors have members with widely varied work experience, the boards are strongest in community and political work experience. The members' high level of participation in other community organizations is undoubtedly a function of the direct effort of the CDC to have organizational representation and linkages throughout the community. The CDC governing boards also contain a higher proportion of poor and less well-educated people than one would find on most citywide governing boards and certainly on the boards of most traditional business and economic institutions. Thus, while the CDC boards of directors do constitute an elite of their communities, the composition of the governing boards still reflects the communities to the extent that most politically constituted governing boards in the United States, particularly nonpartisan ones, do. The CDC governing boards can be considered to be as representative of their communities as most political governing bodies are. The members of these boards are not experts on economic development selected to set policy as experts; rather, they are primarily active, concerned citizens who have chosen to stay within their poverty areas to try to make them better places. They make policy within the framework of improving their communities through economic development rather than making a profit for their economic institutions—though it is hoped by all that eventually the two will not be totally incompatible.

NOTES

1. For a discussion of current definitions and their virtues and vices, see Charles M. Bonjean, Terry N. Clark, and Robert L. Lineberry, eds., *Community Politics: A Behavioral Approach* (New York: Free Press, 1971), especially pp. 1-25.

2. Robert Kennedy's views on this subject can be found in U.S., House Committee on Education and Labor, Hearings on the Economic Opportunity Act of 1964, 88th Cong. 2nd sess., 1964, pp. 207-12, 310-39.

3. *Economic Opportunity Act of 1964* (Washington, D.C.: Government Printing Office, 1965).

4. *Economic Opportunity Act of 1964, Amended through December 23, 1967*, (Washington, D.C.: Government Printing Office, 1968).

5. Ibid.

6. The development of some of these corporations and examples of their operation are discussed in Howard W. Hallman, *Neighborhood Control of Public Programs: Case Studies of Community Corporations and Neighborhood Boards* (New York: Praeger, 1970).

7. Robert A. Nisbet, *The Sociological Tradition* (New York: Basic Books, 1967), pp. 47-48.

8. Suzanne Keller, *The Urban Neighborhood* (New York: Random House, 1968), pp. 99-102.

9. This case is described in Stewart E. Perry, "Black Institutions, Black Separatism, and Ghetto Economic Development," *Human Organization* 31 (Fall 1972): 271-79.

10. Burt Griffin and Zachary Paris, in the preliminary results of their research on non-OEO-funded CDCs, have found a similar pattern. Manuscript in progress, Chapter 13, p. 3.

11. Early attitudes toward stock ownership are found in Robert Kennedy's testimony, U.S., House, Committee on Education and Labor, Hearings on the Economic Opportunity Act of 1964, 88th Cong., 2nd sess., 1964; also Jack Newfield, *Robert Kennedy: A Memoir* (New York: Bantam, 1970). Later views are recorded in Griffin and Paris, Chapter 16.

12. Myles L. Mace, *Directors: Myth and Reality* (Boston: Harvard University Graduate School of Business Administration, 1971).

13. *Corporate Directorship Practices: Studies in Business Policy No. 103* (New York: National Industrial Conference Board, 1962). See Also J. M. Juran and J. Keith Louden, *The Corporate Director* (New York: American Management Association, 1966).

14. The data for computing the size of CDC boards of directors was obtained from either the CDCs themselves or from the OEO analysts responsible for the operation of the CDC in question. The figure on board size represents all the active governing boards operating in the summer of 1973.

15. Griffin and Paris, in the preliminary statement of their findings about CDCs in Cleveland, Ohio, reported similar selection mechanisms. See Griffin and Paris, Chapter 5.

16. Mace, *Directors*, p. 94.

17. Ibid., p. 106.

18. Kenneth Prewitt, *The Recruitment of Political Leaders: A Study of Citizen Politicians* (Indianapolis: Bobbs-Merrill, 1970).

19. Mace, *Directors*; Juran and Louden, *Corporate Director*; Melvin T. Copeland and Andrew R. Towl, *The Board of Directors and Business Management* (New York: Greenwood, 1968).

20. Prewitt, *Recruitment*, p. 4.

21. Harold D. Lasswell and Abraham Kaplan, *Power and Society* (New Haven: Yale University Press, 1950), p. 226.

22. Prewitt, *Recruitment*, p. 14. See also Robert A. Dahl, *Preface to Democratic Theory* (Chicago: University of Chicago Press, 1956).

23. Prewitt, *Recruitment*, p. 47.

24. Howard W. Hallman, *Government By Neighborhoods* (Washington, D.C.: Center for Government Studies, 1973), p. 39.

25. Prewitt, *Recruitment*, p. 133.

26. Charles M. Bonjean, Terry N. Clark, and Robert L. Lineberry, "The Structure of Mass Participation in Community Politics," in *Community Politics*, ed. Bonjean, Clark, and Lineberry, p. 83.

27. Robert R. Alford and Eugene C. Lee, "Voting Turnout in American Cities," in ibid., pp. 87-105.

28. Robert A. Dahl, *Who Governs?* (New Haven: Yale University Press, 1961).

29. Hallman, *Government By Neighborhoods*, p. 39.

30. Daniel P. Moynihan, *Maximum Feasible Misunderstanding: Community Action in the War on Poverty* (New York: Free Press, 1969), p. 137.

31. Ralph M. Kramer, *Participation of the Poor: Comparative Community Case Studies in the War on Poverty* (Englewood Cliffs, N.J.: Prentice-Hall, 1969), p. 197.

32. Alan A. Altshuler, *Community Control: The Black Demand for Participation In Large American Cities* (Indianapolis: Pegasus, 1970), p. 138.

33. Ibid.

34. Sar Levitan, *The Great Society's Poor Law* (Baltimore: Johns Hopkins University Press, 1969), p. 114.

35. Altshuler, *Community Control*, p. 139.

36. For further details see Barry Stein, *The Harlem Commonwealth Council: Business as a Strategy for Community Development* (Cambridge, Mass.: Center for Community Economic Development, 1974).

37. Altshuler, *Community Control*, pp. 140-41.

38. John MacPhee, in *Local Government and Community Autonomy in East Boston* (Cambridge, Mass.: Center for Community Economic Development, 1973), discusses some of the conflicts of interest and pressures board members can feel because of their organizational and occupational affiliations.

39. Dahl, *Preface to Democratic Theory*, pp. 131-32.

40. Prewitt, *Recruitment*, p. 210.

41. Ibid., p. 212.

42. Two fairly readable discussions of this question are William H. Flanigan, *Political Behavior of the American Electorate*, 2nd ed. (Boston: Allyn and Bacon, 1972), and Sidney Verba and Norman M. Nie, *Participation in America: Political Democracy and Social Equality*, (New York: Harper and Row, 1972).

43. See Brian J. Reilly, "Distribution of SIP Funds." *CCED Newsletter*, February 1973.

44. John Kenneth Galbraith, in "Power and the Useful Economist," *American Economic Review*, 63 (March 1973): 1-11, comments on the absence of the concept of community in these theories and in our tradition.

45. John Kenneth Galbraith, *Economics, Peace and Laughter* (New York: Signet, New American Library, 1972), p. 22.

46. Warner Bloomberg, Jr., and Florence W. Rosenstock, "Who Can Activate the Poor? One Assessment of Maximum Feasible Participation," in *Community Politics*, ed. Bonjean, Clark, and Lineberry, p. 150.

47. See Prewitt, *Recruitment*, pp. 36-46. See also Oliver P. Williams, Harold Heiman, Charles S. Liebman, and Thomas R. Dye, *Suburban Differences and Metropolitan Policies: The Philadelphia Story* (Philadelphia: University of Pennsylvania Press, 1964), and Bryan T. Downes, "Municipal Social Rank and the Characteristics of Local Political Leaders," *Midwest Journal of Political Science* 12, no. 4 (November 1968).

4

THE PROCESS OF
CONTROLLING THE
COMMUNITY DEVELOPMENT
CORPORATION

Community development corporations are forums for community self-determination only to the extent that their boards of directors actually direct and control the CDCs for the benefit of their communities. This chapter presents an overview of the functions performed by the board members, the substance of their decision making, and the nature and extent of the limitations imposed upon the boards' powers. The functions performed by the board members of large- and medium-sized business corporations and of city council members in the council-manager form of government are compared with those of the CDC board members to determine more precisely the nature of the "community control" that CDC board members have.

FUNCTIONS OF GOVERNING BOARDS IN GENERAL

Typical Functions of a Board of Directors
of a Business Corporation

Most articles of incorporation state that "the board of directors shall consist of at least three members and shall manage the company." Like many small phrases in legal documents, the phrase "shall manage the company" can have a variety of meanings in practice. According to Myles L. Mace's study of the boards of directors of large- and medium-sized manufacturing, mining, and retailing business corporations, most such boards perform three basic functions: they provide advice and counsel, serve as agents of discipline, and act in crisis situations.[1]

The function of providing advice and counsel to corporation management means, according to Mace, that most boards are not the basic decision-making bodies of their corporations but rather sounding boards and checkpoints for management. While most boards are not simply rubber stamps for management, set up only to mollify stockholders or outsiders, they nevertheless are not the ones who make the final decisions. The advice and counsel given cover such areas as technology, finance, government relations, real estate, agriculture, venture expansion and acquisitions, employee benefits, pension plans, and so on.

The discipline function of the board consists essentially of its review and control of the activities of the corporation management. In this role as the corporate conscience, the board ensures that the executive director and other staff members do their required homework and have thoroughly thought through procedures, proposals, and processes. The importance of this function can be illustrated by the following quotation from one of the executive directors of the corporations that Mace studied:

> The conscience function is involved in capital appropriations, operating budgets, compensation decisions, and others. The board is not really a decision-making body, but it is involved in the decision-making process as a sort of corporate conscience. The board rarely, if ever, rejects out of hand a proposal by the president, but their existence in the management scheme of things influences the president and helps keep his decisions within the bounds of conscionable conduct.[2]

Another major function of the boards of directors of most corporations is the assumption of an active decision-making role during times of crises, particularly when (1) the corporation's director dies or leaves suddenly or (2) the management's performance is unsatisfactory, potentially leading to the failure of the corporation. The three major functions of board members described by Mace are echoed by other studies of the boards of directors of business corporations.[3]

Functions Performed by City Councils

According to some advocates, community control must be implemented by a variation of the city council political entity on a smaller neighborhood scale.[4] The city councils in the council-manager plan of government are the type of city council that is by far the most comparable with the CDC boards being studied. The International City Managers' Association (ICMA) notes that under this system of local government the council "enjoys all the importance and responsibility of a board of directors."[5] The major functions of these councils are described by the ICMA study, and by more analytical studies as

well, as (1) determination of policy for the city, (2) supervision of policy administration and implementation, (3) selection and replacement of a city manager,
and (4) the exercise of public leadership.[6] The fourth function includes review
of existing policies and operations, assistance in the formation and development
of community opinions, and generation of support for community programs
and services.

This brief sketch of the functions of city councils in the council-manager
form of government shows a greater stress on policy and decision making and on
the public leadership functions of these political governing boards than was
found for the governing boards of business corporations. The functions of maintaining discipline by monitoring, review, and control of management and operations and acting in crisis situations to select and replace management are the
same. Part of our task here is to determine, as we did for the recruitment and
selection procedures, whether the CDC governing boards are more similar to
the governing boards of business corporations or to governing boards of political
entities, that is, city councils.

FUNCTIONS OF THE GOVERNING BOARDS OF
COMMUNITY DEVELOPMENT CORPORATIONS

In analyzing the functions performed by the CDC boards of directors,
five categories of functions will be discussed. These are the functions of (1)
providing advice and counsel to management, (2) determining policy for the
CDC, (3) supervising policy administration and implementation, (4) acting in
crisis situations to select and/or replace the executive director, and (5) exercising
public leadership for the CDC. The last four are functions of city councils, while
the first, third, and fourth are functions of the boards of businesses.

Because experience can be a factor in determining both the type of
functions performed and the quality of performance, the basic analytical categories of geographical location and amount of funds the CDC had received from
OEO were first examined to see if the board members varied significantly in
the lengths of time they had been board members. The data in Table 4.1 reveal
that they do not: about 60 percent of all members have been in office 2 years
or less. The chairpersons also do not vary significantly among themselves, but
in all instances they differ considerably from the members in terms of lengths
of time as board members. Overall, about 63 percent of the chairpersons have
been on the board 25 months or more, although not necessarily in their present
position, while only 33 percent of the board members have been members that
long. Thus, experience on the board, seems to be an important factor in the
selection of board chairpersons.

For our immediate purposes it is important to note that the CDCs do not
vary significantly in terms of the number of years a member has been in office,
by either geographical location or the amount of funds the CDC has received

TABLE 4.1

Length of Time on Board
(in percent)

	24 Months or Less	25 Months or Less	No Response
Rural			
Chairpersons (N = 9)	22	78	0
Members (N = 108)	58	32	10
Urban			
Chairpersons (N = 10)	50	50	0
Members (N = 165)	61	34	5
Total			
Chairpersons (N = 19)	37*	63*	0
Members (N = 273)	60*	33*	7
In corporations of			
Less than $2 million			
Chairpersons (N = 13)	38	62	0
Members (N = 193)	62	32	6
$2 million or more			
Chairpersons (N = 6)	33	66	0
Members (N = 80)	58	35	7

* p for the chi square test < .05.
Source: The author's 1973 survey of CDC board members.

from OEO. Hence the responses to the questions concerning the functions performed by the members, when analyzed within these two major categories, should not be affected by the personal experience factors of the individual members.

Although attendance at board meetings is not usually mentioned as a major function of governing boards, it obviously is a necessary prerequisite for effective participation. For this reason, both the Abt and the Kelly questionnaires inquired about attendance. Abt Associates asked the respondents to indicate the percentage of meetings attended, referring essentially to the months of September to June. As Table 4.2 shows, the responses to this question revealed sharp differences between rural and urban board members. While 62 percent of the rural board members had attended 91 percent or more of the meetings, only 46 percent of the urban members had attended this many. Nonetheless, the percentage of members attending 70 percent or fewer was small; 15 percent for urban members and 7 percent for rural members. Although more urban chairpersons had attended 91 percent or more of the meetings than did the urban members (62 percent to 46 percent), these chairpersons had attended a substantially lower percentage than the rural chairpersons. The latter said they had attended 100 percent of all meetings. The Kelly survey asked how many meetings the respondents had attended in the last three months, essentially June to September. (All CDCs have at least one meeting each month.) No significant differences in attendance during these months were found— 67 percent of the members and 74 percent of the chairpersons attended three or more meetings. On the basis of attendance, it would appear that only about two-thirds of the CDC board members and about three-fourths of the CDC board chairpersons are constant participants in the governing of their CDCs. The governing boards in rural areas tend to have slightly higher levels of participation by both the chairpersons and the members.

Data from the Abt 1972 survey indicated that 65 percent of the members and 92 percent of the chairpersons said they performed functions for the CDC in addition to attending monthly board meetings. In the pretest for the Kelly survey, it was found that the general question about functions performed was as often as not equated with whether or not the person was a member of a board

TABLE 4.2

Percent of Meetings Attended

	No Response	70 percent or Less	71-90 Percent	91-100 Percent
Rural				
Chairpersons[a] (N = 11)	0	0	0	100
Members[b] (N = 162)	2	7	28	62
Urban				
Chairpersons[a] (N = 13)	15	8	15	62
Members[b] (N = 178)	4	15	35	46
Total				
Chairpersons[b] (N = 24)	8	4	8	79
Members[b] (N = 340)	3	11	32	54
Total OEO funding				
Less than $2 million				
Chairpersons (N = 12)	8	8	0	83
Members (N = 184)	2	10	29	59
$2 million or more				
Chairpersons (N = 12)	8	0	17	75
Members (N = 156)	5	18	35	47

[a] p for the Fisher Exact one-tailed test < .13.

[b] p for chi square test < .05.

Source: Author's analysis of 1972 Abt survey data on CDC board members and chairpersons.

committee or chairperson of a committee. Hence the general question was changed, and the board members first asked whether they felt that they held special positions on the board. As Table 4.3 shows, the overall percentage of board members stating they were committee chairmen, officers, or members was about the same as the total for the Abt survey stating they did something in addition to attending regular board meetings (64 percent to 65 percent). About one-third of all members surveyed in 1973 were committee chairpersons or officers; another third were committee members; and another third were simply board members. The participation is unaffected by the CDC's location or level of funding. These data suggest that about two-thirds of most CDC boards tend to formulate policy and discuss it in depth.

TABLE 4.3

Members Holding Special Positions on the Boards
(in percent)

	Committee Chairperson or CDC Officer	Committee Member	No Special Position
Rural (N = 108)	32	29	39
Urban (N = 165)	36	30	33
Total (N = 273)	34	30	35
In corporation of			
Less than $2 million (N = 193)	35	29	36
$2 million or more (N = 80)	34	33	34

Source: The author's 1973 survey of CDC board members.

Providing Advice and Counsel to Management

Two specific questions in the Abt survey pertain to the performance of the function of providing advice and counsel to management. (See Table 4.4.) The results show that about 77 percent of the chairpersons and 37 percent of the other board members perform this function. On the more technical matter of performing venture feasibility studies, a much lower proportion of the chairpersons and members (only 14 percent of each group) indicated that they were actively involved.

Determining Policy for the CDC

One of the key differences between the governing boards of most business corporations and those of most cities is the scope and nature of their respective

TABLE 4.4

Percentage Providing Advice and Counsel to Management

| | Rural | | Urban | | Total | | Total OEO Funding | | | |
| | | | | | | | Less than $2 million | | $2 million or More | |
	Chair-persons (N = 11)	Members (N = 162)	Chair-persons (N = 13)	Members (N = 178)	Chair-persons (N = 24)	Members (N = 340)	Chair-persons (N = 12)	Members (N = 184)	Chair-persons (N = 12)	Members (N = 156)
Provide advice to director and professional staff										
Yes	73	33	82	40	77	37	91	34	64	39
No	27	29	18	28	23	28	9	23	36	33
No response	0	39	0	33	0	36	0	42	0	28
Perform venture feasibility studies										
Yes	18	15	9	12	14	14	17	15	8	12
No	82	46	91	54	86	51	75	43	83	60
No response	0	39	0	33	0	36	8	42	8	28

Source: Author's analysis of 1972 Abt survey data on CDC board numbers and chairpersons.

decision-making powers. One of the central debates over the long-term viability of community economic development is whether or not the stated ideal of community control of the movement is a handicap or an asset to economic development in poverty environments. For example, J. A. C. Hetherington, a Wisconsin Law professor, contends that the goal of community control is fundamentally opposed to the goal of profit.[7] At the core of this debate is the issue of the extent to which the CDC governing boards ought to exercise the policy-making function. Some observers fear that community control necessarily spells doom to the profit motive and to the establishment of prosperous and self-sufficient business enterprises.

In political bodies, control in the policy-making area usually involves major attention to the delivery of services to residents. In economic units such control, which normally resides in the private, not the public, "community" sector is concerned with profit. As Mace points out, most boards of directors of business corporations are not the ultimate decision makers in most situations. In the political area, however, city council members usually are. For the CDCs this issue will be addressed by assessing the overall policy-making power of the board members compared with that of external sources, such as a funding agency like OEO, and that of internal CDC forces, such as the executive director. This process should make it clear whether the CDC governing board is more like that of a business corporation or that of a city council in its fulfillment of the policy-making function.

Scope of the Boards' Policy-Making Powers: An Overview

In theory the CDC boards of directors are expected to be the chief determiners of policy for their CDCs. In the Abt survey, the participating board members were asked to indicate whether or not they believed this to be true. The specific question was, "In general, how much influence do you think the following groups or persons actually have in determining the policies and actions of the CDC?" The members were asked to rate the influence of each group specified in Table 4.5 by giving a "1" to those of primary influence on all issues, a "2" to those who have much influence on almost all issues, a "3" to those who have much influence on some issues, a "4" to those who have some influence, and a "5" to those having little or no influence. The data in Table 4.5 show that the CDC board members do not tend to think of themselves as the chief determiners of the policies and actions of the CDCs. The members place the influence of both the Office of Economic Opportunity and the executive directors above their own. The chairpersons do not differ from the members in this tendency.

The data in Table 4.6, which gives a more detailed percentage breakdown of the members' responses, reveal several variations among the CDCs by urban-rural location and by the amount of funds received from OEO. First, the rural

TABLE 4.5

Perceptions of Relative Influence in Determining Policies and Actions

| | Rural | | Urban | | Total | | Total OEO Funding | | | |
| | | | | | | | Less Than $2 million | | $2 Million or More | |
	Chairpersons (N = 8)	Members (N = 162)	Chairpersons (N = 9)	Members (N = 178)	Chairpersons (N = 17)	Members (N = 340)	Chairpersons (N = 8)	Members (N = 184)	Chairpersons (N = 9)	Members (N = 156)
Executive Director	2.38	1.81	2.13	2.17	2.25	2.00	2.43	2.13	2.11	1.79
OEO	2.38	2.15	2.13	2.17	2.25	2.16	2.43	2.15	2.11	2.18
CDC board	2.50	2.38	3.13	2.27	2.69	2.32	3.00	2.43	2.44	2.19
CDC executive committee	4.33	2.32	3.55	2.77	3.86	2.58	3.60	2.70	4.00	2.29
CDC professional staff	3.38	2.52	3.14	2.83	3.27	2.68	4.00	2.71	2.78	2.64

Source: Author's analysis of 1972 Abt survey data on CDC board members and chairpersons.

TABLE 4.6

Chi-Square Analyses of Relative Influence in Determining Policies and Actions (in percent)

| | Rural | | Urban | | Total | | Total OEO Funding | | | |
| | | | | | | | Less than $2 Million | | $2 million or More | |
	Chair-persons (N = 8)	Members (N = 162)	Chair-persons (N = 9)	Members (N = 178)	Chair-persons (N = 17)	Members (N = 340)	Chair-persons (N = 8)	Members (N = 184)	Chair-persons (N = 9)	Members (N = 156)
Influence of OEO										
1 or 2 rating										
primary or much	63	62	56	59	59	60	50	60	67	61
Other	37	26	33	29	35	28	38	38	33	36
Don't Know/										
no answer	0	12	11	12	6	12	13	3	0	3
Influence of director										
1	13	36[a]	22[a]	25	18	31	25	23[a]	11	40
2	50	43[a]	44[a]	31	47	41	63	42[a]	89	40

Other	38	13[a]	22[a]	38	29	22	0	28[a]	0	15[a]
Don't know/ no answer	0	7	11	6	6	7	13	8	0	6
Influence of professional staff										
1 or 2 rating	25	52[a]	22	34[a]	24	42	0[b]	37	44[b]	49
Other	75	37[a]	56	51[a]	64	45	75[b]	46	56[b]	42
Don't know/ no answer	0	11	22	15	12	13	25	17	0	9
Influence of CDC board										
1 or 2 rating	63	54	44	60	53	57	38	54	67	60
Other	38	36	44	34	41	35	50	37	33	33
Don't know/ no answer	0	10	11	6	6	8	13	9	0	7
Influence of CDC executive committee										
1 and 2 Rating	0	35[a]	11	23[a]	6	29	13	33[a]	0	24[a]
Other	38	15[a]	33	26[a]	35	21	50	32[a]	22	8[a]
Don't know/ no answer	63	50	55	51	59	50	38	35	78	69

[a] p for Chi Square test < .05.
[b] p for Fisher Extract 1-tailed test = .09.
Source: Author's analysis of 1972 Abt survey data on CDC board members and chairpersons.

CDC board members rate the influence of their executive directors significantly higher than the urban members do; 79 percent of the rural members give them a "1" or "2" rating, but only 56 percent of the urban members do. In addition, thr rural members give a significantly higher rating to the influence of the professional staff (52 percent to 34 percent). The rural members also rate the influence of the executive committees higher (35 percent to 23 percent). Generally speaking, the chairpersons rate the influence of the directors and the professional staffs lower than the other members do.

The differences found between the CDCs in terms of the amount of funds received from OEO are that the members of the wealthier CDCs rate the influence of the executive director and the executive committees higher than the members of the less well-funded CDCs, while the chairpersons of the wealthier CDCs rate the influence of the professional staff higher than the chairpersons of the less well-funded CDCs. (See Table 4.6.)

In my 1974 study of CDC executive directors based upon comparable Abt data, it was found that in general the directors also felt that they were the chief determiners of CDC policies and actions. Most directors indicated that the CDC board had more influence then OEO, however. The rural directors tended to be less inclined to rate themselves as the primary determiners of CDC policy than the urban directors were. More of the directors of the wealthier CDCs gave their professional staffs a "1" or "2" rating on the influence scale than gave "1" or "2" ratings to their own boards of directors. Of these directors, 88 percent gave the professional staffs these high ratings while 50 percent gave their boards the high ratings.[8]

The important fact to note here is not that the directors and the board members of the various subgroupings do or do not agree on the relative amounts of influence of specific groups, but rather than both do agree that the CDC boards of directors are *not* the chief determiners of the policies and actions of the CDC. Does this finding mean that the community control aspect of the community economic development movement is simply an ideological nicety? We will have to return to this question later, after the specific external and internal limitations placed upon the boards are examined in greater detail. At this point, however, it can be concluded that in terms of the nature and scope of their policy-making functions the CDC governing boards are more comparable with the governing boards of most business corporations than with those of cities. Therefore community control over a community development corporation is of a quite different and of a less comprehensive nature than the control that exists in cities under the council-manager form of government.

The fact that the CDC governing board does not hold primacy in the policy-making area even in the eyes of its own members stands in sharp contrast to the findings of Ronald Loveridge in his study of the roles of city managers in legislative politics in the 87 San Francisco Bay Area cities. He found that city council members definitely believe they have that primacy. The difference in the board members' perceptions of the roles of their respective governing boards in policy making can be seen by comparing Table 4.7 with Table 4.6. Fewer than 10 percent of the city council members thought the city manager initiated most or all policy matters, while the majority (58 percent) thought the city council was dominant in this area. Loveridge also points out elsewhere that only 14 percent of the city councilmen felt that the city executive should be a policy leader, while only 48 percent thought the city manager should even propose policies or solutions.[9]

It must be noted, however, that studies of actual policy making demonstrate that even city managers, who are prohibited by legal and symbolic traditions from being dominant political leaders, do tend to become such leaders in many instances. The reasons this happens in the council-manager form of government are not very different from the reasons why the chief executive officers of CDCs tend to become dominant. The city manager has a near monopoly on information about what is actually happening in policy administration; part-time city councilmen cannot maintain the same level of knowledge. Further, an executive cannot successfully implement policy without being intimately involved in the policy-making process. In addition, city managers also see themselves as problem solvers, innovators, and doers, not just as housekeepers. This self-perception propels them into the policy-making area. Perhaps the most critical factor leading to policy participation and dominance is the special training and expertise that the executive officer brings to the job. Few governing board members, whether those of a CDC or of a city, can match that training and expertise.

TABLE 4.7

City Council Members' Perceptions of Initiation of Policy Matters
(in percent)

	Members (N = 293)
Manager initiates all policy matters	1
Manager initiates most policy matters	9
Manager and council equally initiate policy matters	31
Council initiates most policy matters	25
Council initiates all policy matters	33

Table reproduced from *City Managers in Legislative Politics* by Ronald O. Loveridge, copyright (c) 1971, by The Bobbs-Merrill Company, Inc., reprinted by permission of the publisher.

Source: Ronald O. Loveridge, *City Managers in Legislative Politics* (Indianapolis: Bobbs-Merrill, 1971), p. 142.

Types of Decisions Made by Boards of Community Development Corporations

Although it is evident that the CDC governing boards do not consider themselves the basic determiners of CDC policies, they do have the right of final approval on all policies. To obtain an idea of the types of decisions the boards actually do make, the Kelly survey asked the members to indicate the three most important decisions their boards had made in the past year. (See Table 4.8.)

In the opinions of the board members, the most important decisions made by their boards substantively involved four topics: establishing an overall strategy for the CDC; setting goals for the year; determining the general kinds of businesses to invest in; and making "go, no go" decisions about specific ventures, loans, and investments. These four topics, selected by the largest

TABLE 4.8

The Three Most Important Decisions:
Views of Members and Chairpersons
(in percent)

	Placed Item Among Top Three	
Decisions	Members (N = 273)	Chairpersons (N = 19)
Establishing an overall strategy	48	68
Setting goals for the year	47	53
Determining the general kinds of businesses to invest in	49[a]	47
Making "go, no go" decisions about specific ventures, loans, and investments	42	37
Choosing the executive director	18[b]	16
Changing the executive director	13	11
Requesting more funds and/or time from a funding source such as OEO	31	26
Investing in a Minority Enterprise Small Business Investment Company (MESBIC)	6	5
Establishing or revising personnel policies and procedures	26	21

[a] A significantly higher proportion of the members from the CDCs receiving less than $2 million (52 percent) included this item among the top three, compared with the members from CDCs receiving more than $2 million (42 percent).

[b] A significantly higher proportion of the rural members (28 percent) included this item among the top three, compared to the urban members (12 percent). No other significant differences appeared in the subanalyses.

Source: The author's 1973 survey of CDC board members and chairpersons.

proportion of board members and chairpersons, tend to concern basic policy-level and planning types of decisions that are directly related to the boards' essential task of directing the CDCs for the benefit of their communities. The decisions selected by 31 percent or fewer of the board members generally involve the basic structural and procedural problems of the CDC itself as an institution. This latter type of decision, such as choosing or changing a director, requesting more funds or time, or establishing or revising personnel policies and procedures, concerns matters primarily involving implementation. They are control functions and startup problems which all CDCs face at some point.

The responses of the board members to this question about the most important decisions they make suggest that the board members feel that they do make some of the most critical policy decisions for their CDCs, even though the majority feel that OEO and the CDC executive directors have a greater overall influence on CDC policies than they do.

External Limitations on the Board's Decision-making Powers

In Chapter 2, when the objectives of the CDC board members were discussed, it was pointed out that because the CDCs are funded by OEO as part of a community economic development program, certain goals must be set. In other words, an external force that has the financial resources to support or kill the CDC obviously restricts the decision-making powers of the board. If funds are not to be cut off, policies can be set only within the existing federal framework.

There are several ways in which external forces can limit these decision-making powers. For example, most CDCs are incorporated as nonprofit, charitable organizations. Because they thus qualify as tax-exempt organizations that receive tax-deductible donations under Section 501 (c) (3) of the Internal Revenue Code, these CDCs are restrained from lobbying and direct political involvement. Nonetheless, the CDCs are directly affected by politicians. Should a U.S. Senator or member of Congress oppose the CDC and its goals, several federal programs of potential support for the CDC could be closed off. Conversely, if the politician strongly support the CDC, then doors could more easily be opened.

Even such a basic decision as the selection of the areas of economic development in which to work can be determined by the existence or lack of federal, regional, or state funds. For example, without the financial and technical support of such housing agencies as the Department of Housing and Urban Development, the Farmer's Home Administration, and the Federal Housing Authority, almost no CDC could even consider entering the field of housing development and rehabilitation. Because such funds and programs do exist, however, CDCs often do choose housing development as a central objective. Once this choice is made and involvement with these agencies is contracted,

TABLE 4.9

Board Response: Do Office of Economic Opportunity Policies Constrain Boards?
(in percent)

| | Rural | | Urban | | Total | | Total OEO Funding | | | |
| | | | | | | | Less than $2 Million | | $2 Million or More | |
	Chairpersons (N=11)	Members (N=162)	Chairpersons (N=13)	Members (N=178)	Chairpersons (N=24)	Members (N=340)	Chairpersons (N=12)	Members (N=184)	Chairpersons (N=12)	Members (N=156)
Does OEO place constraints?										
Yes	36	56[a]	46	43[a]	42	49	33	53	50	45
No	36	36[a]	23	52[a]	29	45	33	42	25	47
No response	27	7	31	4	29	6	33	4	25	8
On OEO/OED venture approval procedures										
Yes	36	44[a]	31	26[a]	33	34	33	35	33	33
No	0	12[a]	15	16[a]	8	14	0	16	17	11
No response	64	44	54	58	58	52	67	48	50	56

ON OEO/OED-sponsored technical assistance										
Yes	18	14	23	12	21	13	25	13	17	12
No	18	41	23	30	21	36	8	39	33	32
No response	64	45	54	58	58	52	67	48	50	56
On policy issuances and guidelines										
Yes	36	31	23	26	29	29	33	27	25	31
No	0	24	23	15	13	19	0	26	25	12
No response	64	44	54	59	58	52	67	48	50	57
On policies concerning board composition										
Yes	9	10[a]	15	16[a]	13	13	25[b]	13	0[b]	13
No	27	45[a]	31	26[a]	29	35	8[b]	39	50[b]	31
No response	64	44	54	58	58	52	67	48	50	56
On release-of-funds mechanisms										
Yes	27	31	31	26	29	29	33	29	25	28
No	9	24	15	16	13	20	0	23	25	16
No response	64	44	54	58	58	52	67	48	50	56

[a] p for Chi Square Test < .05.

[b] p for Fisher Exact Test = .033.

Source: Author's analysis of 1972 Abt survey data on CDC board members and chairpersons.

91

other decisions are also circumscribed. The Federal Housing Authority can require specific numbers of rooms and units and set the mortgage fees and rents.

For the CDCs included in this study, the Office of Economic Opportunity was the most salient external force having the potential for constraining the boards' decision-making power. In the Abt survey the board members were asked whether or not they felt OEO policies or procedures place constraints on their boards' ability to operate effectively. About one-half (49 percent) of all 340 respondents said yes; 45 percent, however, said no. (See Table 4.9.) As the data in Table 4.9 show, the largest percentage (34 percent) of members said the constraints on venture approval procedures were the ones most reducing their ability to operate effectively. This finding is not unexpected, since a strong movement had been in existence for some time to have OEO give the CDCs autonomy over the selection and monitoring of their ventures. As noted in Chapter 1, in 1974 OEO finally agreed to permit those CDCs it judges to have been successful to have final authority over venture approval. About 29 percent of all the board members said that the OEO mechanisms for the release of funds and for general policy issuances and guidelines were constraining effective operation. Only 13 percent of the members felt OEO policy on technical assistance or on the composition of the board of directors was adversely affecting their boards' ability to operate effectively.

In general the rural board members reacted more negatively to OEO policies than did the urban members. A significantly higher proportion felt that the OEO imposed constraints (56 percent to 43 percent) and considered the OEO venture approval procedures particularly harmful (44 percent to 26 percent). The urban members, however, were significantly more upset then the rural members about the OEO policies concerning the compositions of boards of directors (16 percent to 10 percent). As was pointed out in Chapter 3, the urban CDCs tend not to have open elections and to seek community involvement by organizational representation instead. They also are more likely to have closed memberships than the rural CDCs. These arrangements do not fit the conceptions of community economic development of several OEO (now CSA) personnel. The chairpersons vary only in that the chairpersons of the less-funded CDCs have a higher percentage that say the OEO policies on board composition impede effective board operations. (See Table 4.9.) The amount of funds the CDC receives from OEO appear to make no significant difference in whether or not the board members feel constrained by OEO.

In sum, the relationships of most CDC boards with OEO (CSA) appear to be somewhat tense. Constraints are obviously felt, some quite strongly. To date no one has yet found a way to resolve the ambiguity of the situation. On the one hand the boards of directors are expected to act as decision makers for community-controlled and theoretically community-owned property and investments. On the other hand, since these investments are made with OEO or other federal agency funds that can be cut off or, if need be, even forcibly returned to the government, the CDC boards are expected to act as local representatives of the federal government. To the extent that the local boards agree with the overall objectives of the OEO community economic development program, it would seem that the conflicts and constraints would be minimized.

It could be argued that city councils are subject to similar restrictions when they deal with federal agencies. To some extent this is true, but city councils have a greater range of choices among federal programs. Only one federal agency, CSA, funds CDCs at any meaningful level. Most federal as well as state agencies have numerous programs for city rather than neighborhood needs. Moreover, city councils have the power to tax residents. The reality of community control at the neighborhood level has never included this possibility, even though some theorists, like Milton Kotler, have advocated it.[10] In any case, an institution such as a CDC would have to be designated as a governmental unit to have this option.

Internal Limitations Placed upon the Board's Decision-making Powers

The external limitations on the CDC boards of directors derive from the fact that the financial power and ultimate control of the CDC resources do not initially reside within the corporation itself, but rather must be won through demonstrated competence. The internal limitations, which reflect this need to be competent in the eyes of outsiders, are directly connected with the relationship of the board to the CDC staff and director.

The Abt survey asked the board members to indicate their perception of their boards' influence relative to the influence of staff in five selected CDC processes. The results in Table 4.10 show that the board members perceive that they themselves have the greatest influence on CDC project and venture investment decisions: 56 percent of the members said they thought the board had very much influence; 30 percent thought it had some influence; and only 7 percent said it had little or no influence. The members also perceived their influence on goal selection and strategy design as high: 40 percent said they had very much influence, 34 percent said some influence, and 10 percent said little or no influence.

The fact that the board members' perceived influence on goal selection and strategy design is lower than their perceived influence on CDC project and venture investment decisions might well be the result of the framework OEO funding imposes upon the goals of the CDC. The environmental facts of poverty areas also tend to constrain the strategies open to economic developers. For example, ordinarily it would not be advisable, to try to concentrate on the building of factories requiring highly skilled laborers. The lack of ready and sufficient capital and the superabundance of unskilled labor limit the strategies that can be selected.

The board members were also asked to indicate the extent of their influence on CDC staff hiring and promotion. As Table 4.10 reveals, only

TABLE 4.10

Board Perception of Its Influence Relative to
Staff in Selected Processes
(in percent)

	Chairpersons (N = 24)	Members (N = 340)
Goal selection and strategy design		
Very much influence	54	49
Some influence	46	34
Little or no influence	0	10
No response	0	7
CDC project and venture investment decisions		
Very much influence	54	56
Some influence	33	30
Little or no influence	13	7
No response	0	7
CDC staff hiring and promotion		
Very much influence	21	29
Some influence	33	31
Little or no influence	46	30
No response	0	10
Venture management and technical assistance procedures		
Very much influence	38	34
Some influence	46	40
Little or no influence	17	15
No response	0	10
Venture staff hiring and promotion		
Very much influence	17	22
Some influence	33	26
Little or no influence	38	33
No response	13	19
Do board members participate equally in decision-making?		
Yes	67	58
No	29	37
No response	4	5

Note: Statistical analyses on the subgroups (by geographical location and funding) found no significant differences.

Source: Author's analysis of 1972 Abt survey data on CDC board members and chairpersons.

29 percent of the members felt they had very much influence; 31 percent said they had some influence; and 30 percent said they had little or no influence. The chairpersons felt they had less influence on these matters than the others examined. It would appear that most CDC executive directors have strong managerial control over their staffs, that the staff is accountable to the director, who in turn is accountable to the board.

The above three items deal with the influence of the CDC boards of directors on their own CDCs. The other two substantive items in Table 4.10 concern the CDC board members' influence on the subsidiary ventures developed by the CDC. Only 33 percent of the board members thought they had very much influence on venture managment and technical assistance procedures, while another 40 percent thought they had some influence. Even less influence was perceived on venture staff hiring and promotion: 33 percent of the board members believed they had little or no influence on these matters.

On the basis of these data one can conclude that the influence of the CDC board members on CDC decisions decreases as the specificity and technical nature of the problem increases.

An Overall Profile of Board-Staff Relationships

To obtain on overall profile of the relationships existing between the CDC boards, their directors, and their staffs, a series of questions developed by Rensis Likert to assess the general nature and level of participation and interaction within business organizations was adapted and used in the Kelly survey.[11] Likert's research is based on the proposition that the greater the interaction, the greater the participation, and that the more the motivation to work is based on reward rather than punishment, the more successful (profitable) a business organization will be. The questions were used in this study to determine the extent of participation of the board in CDC activities and to obtain information on the following variables: (1) the interaction process of the board, the staff, and the director; (2) the nature of the motivational forces used in getting the board members and the CDC staff involved and working; (3) the nature of the communication processes operating; (4) the nature of the decision-making processes; (5) the nature of the goal-setting processes; and (6) the nature of the processes used by the board to control the performance of the CDC organization.

The profile of the overall relationship of the CDC boards of directors to their CDCs resulting from the responses to these questions is presented in Table 4.11. The solid line through the responses depicts the average score (the mean) for all board members. The broken line depicts the average score on each item for the board chairpersons. The dotted line depicts the average score on each item for the directors. The responses are scored from 1 to 20. Those close to the "1" end of the scales indicate that the CDC organization is strongly

TABLE 4.11

Profile of the Board and the CDC Organizational Characteristics

Index	Board Weak		Board Strong	
Leadership interaction				
1. How free do the CDC staff members feel to talk to the board members about their jobs?	Not very free	Slightly free	Quite free	Very free
2. How free does the executive director feel to talk to board members about his job?	Not very free	Slightly free	Quite free	Very free
3. Are staff members' ideas sought and used in making board decisions?	Not very often	Sometimes	Usually	Almost always
Motivational forces used				
4. In trying to increase involvement and output of other board members and of the CDC staff, do board members stress primarily...	Economic security	Status and achievement	New experiences, pride	CDC and community needs
5. Who on the board feels the most responsibility for achieving the CDC's goals?	Mostly the directors not the board	Mostly the Board Chairpersons	Chairpersons and few others	Almost all
Communication processes				
6. How much do you talk with CDC staff (including the director) about achieving CDC goals?	Very little	Little	Quite a bit	A great deal
7. How accurate is the communication from the staff to the board?	Often wrong	Sometimes wrong	Usually accurate	Accurate
8. How well does the board know the problems faced by the staff?	Very little	Some	Quite well	Very well

0   20

Decision-making processes

9. Who on the board really makes the most important policy decisions?

| Mostly the director, not the board | Board chairpersons | Chairpersons and few other members | Almost all the board |

10. Who on the board has the technical and professional knowledge that is generally used in decision-making (excluding consultants)?

| CDC staff, not the board | Board chairpersons | Chairpersons and few others | Almost all the board |

11. Does the way your board makes decisions make the board members want to work harder to achieve CDC goals?

| Not usually | Yes, a little | Yes, some | Yes, a lot |

Goal-setting processes

12. How are your CDC's goals established?

| Orders by board | Orders by board and director | Orders after talks with staff | By group action of all |

13. How much do staff (including the director) resist board-set goals and decisions?

| Very great deal | Quite a bit | Some | Very little |

Quality Control

14. How concentrated are the review and control functions (for evaluating employee and venture performance)?

| In hands of director only | Director, board chairperson only | Director, chairperson, and a few others | Director, plus almost all of board |

15. What does the CDC board use cost, productivity, and other control data for?

| Nothing | Policing staff | Reward and punishment | Reward and some self-guidance | Problem solving |

Note: The solid line represents the average score for the board members who responded; the broken line represents the average score for the board chairmen who responded; the dotted line represents the average scores for the executive directors.

Source: The author's 1973 survey of CDC board members, chairpersons, and executive directors. The general form for this profile was modified from Form S in Appendix II in *The Human Organization: Its Management and Value* by Rensis Likert. Copyright 1967 by McGraw-Hill, Inc. Used by permission of McGraw-Hill Book Company and the author. No further use, reproduction, or distribution of Form S is authorized.

dominated by the director in the eyes of the person(s) responding. Responses between 6 and 10 indicate that the board members are participating slightly, but mostly through their board chairpersons. The responses between 11 and 15 indicate that several board members are at least actively consulted and are participating in the CDC organization on a somewhat equal footing with the director. The responses between 16 and 10 indicate that the board members are definitely and strongly participating in decision-making and organizational activities.

The solid line in Table 4.11 shows that in the opinion of the average board member the CDC boards of directors tend to participate in CDC decision-making and processes through the board chairmen and a few others. As the indices show, the members' average response is lowest on the communication items. They appear to feel particularly weak in their knowledge of the problems facing the CDC staffs than they do on any other item. Their response is also somewhat low on the index of decision making. Although they are inclined to think that participation in decision making is by the chairperson and a few other members, their overall rating for the board's possession of the technical and professional knowledge that is generally used in decision making is about two points lower, as is the members' rating on the effect the board's decision-making procedures have on their desire to work harder to achieve CDC goals. In other words, the members seem to feel that a few members are making the decisions for the board.

The executive directors' responses (indicated by the dotted line in Table 4.11) tend to be consistently different from the board chairpersons' and board members' responses, but closer to the former. As the response to the first three items reveals, the directors are much more optimistic about the positive aspects of the leadership interaction processes than either the board chairpersons or board members, particularly the latter. The board members are not nearly so convinced as the directors that the CDC staffs and the directors themselves feel free to talk to them about their jobs; nor do the board members and chairpersons seem convinced that the staff members' ideas are used in the boards' decision-making processes.

The executive directors, however, are much more negative than the board members and chirpersons when it comes to the nature of the motivational forces used to get people working and with regard to who feels the most responsibility for achieving CDC goals. While the board members and chairpersons rather strongly indicate that they think they are motivated by community needs and the CDC goals, the directors tend to think the motivation is involvement in new experiences and personal pride. The directors do not seem to think the members are as altruistic as the members think they are. The directors are inclined to think that only a few people on their boards have a real sense of responsibility about achieving CDC goals.

The directors score much higher on the communication index than the board members do. As one would expect, they rate the accuracy of the information they give the board quite highly. Nevertheless, everyone seems to agree that the board members do not know the problems faced by the CDC staff very well. This is the only item in the entire profile on which the three groups seem to be in complete agreement.

The decision-making items produced some ambivalence among the directors. Although they judged the technical and professional knowledge of the board members lower than the members themselves did, the directors, more than any other group, rated the boards highest on the item, "Who makes the most important policy decisions?" The directors said almost all the board members make the important decisions. The members were more inclined to think that a relatively few members make the really important decisions.

The directors take an intermediate stand between the chairpersons and the members in terms of whether or not the existing decision-making processes incline the board members to work harder. One might expect this. It is the chairpersons first and then the directors who probably have the greatest impact on the nature of the boards' decision-making processes. If these processes are to be criticized, one would not expect the chairpersons and the directors to be the most inclined to do so.

The directors also rate the goal-setting processes quite high in terms of the extent of staff and board participation. Much more than the board members, the directors believe the staffs offer little resistance to policies set by the boards.

The directors also consider the participation in quality control high. This is somewhat surprising given the lower scores found on the question concerning the technical and professional knowledge of the CDC board. Evaluating employee and venture preformance can be a complicated task. Perhaps the directors are reflecting a division of labor whereby they and a select few of the board, along with appropriate staff, make the technical evaluations and the board reviews the findings of that quality control process.

In sum, it seems evident that when the directors are asked to give profiles of the interelationships between the CDC staffs and their boards, the result is a different picture in terms of emphasis from that given by the board members and chairpersons. The chairpersons will usually be in greater agreement with the director than the average board member. Overall, one would have to conclude that the participation and involvement of board members is not as great as it could be. In the next chapter we will address the question of whether the amount and type of participation makes any difference to CDC success.

Supervision of Policy Administration and Implementation

Of the 273 board members participating in the Kelly survey, 172 were asked to be more spcific with regard to the discipline, review, and control functions they performed. (See Chapter 1 for a discussion of the possible biases of this smaller sample.) As Table 4.12 shows, only slightly more than one-third of all these 172 board members indicated that they review the quarterly monitoring reports or applications being sent to funding agencies. Only 37 percent of the larger group of 273 board members had indicated that they reviewed the reports before they were actually sent. These reports often represent basic policy statements and set objectives for the CDC for various time periods. One can only conclude that the majority of the board members are not actively involved in at least this essential part of the board's function of reviewing policy implementation and maintaining control over the quality of work performed by the staff. On only one item, that of reviewing the progress of the CDC in meeting milestones, schedules, and objectives, did more than half of the 172 members (60 percent) say they were involved. Close to one-half of the members (48 percent) indicated involvement in performing and reviewing the results of venture feasibility studies. A significantly higher proportion of rural compared to urban members review the quarterly monitoring reports sent to OEO—42 percent to 27 percent. Chairpersons are clearly more likely to perform review and control functions than board members are. (See Table 4.12.)

Acting in Crisis Situations:
Selecting and Replacing the Executive Director

When the simpler methods of reviewing and questioning CDC management fail, a crisis develops. Supervision of policy administration ultimately means, Can the board effectively check and control the executive director if and when the need arises? In other words, can the CDC governing boards effectively perform the function of acting decisively in crisis situations? No survey data on this question are available, but careful study of two situations in which one or more board members felt that the chief executive officer needed to be replaced provides some insights.

A crisis situation involving the performance of the executive director is by far the most difficult one a board ever faces. Except for those members who are employed by the CDC, the board is usually handicapped by a lack of access to information independent of the executive director's control concerning the corporations's activities and performance. Hence it may take many months for the board members to discover that management performance is poor. By the time the members learn of the poor performance, it may not be possible to save the corporation. Since most board members have full-time jobs elsewhere and are usually active in other community organizations, they have little time to delve into management's performance. The board members who are employees of the corporation, while more likely to know about poor performance, are handicapped as well. As subordinates of the executive director, they can be accused of insubordination by the director and fired. Nonetheless, it is during these crises that the board must necessarily assume the decision-making powers of the corporation if that corporation is to continue to survive.

TABLE 4.12

Performance of the Review and Control Functions
(in percent)

Function	Rural Chairpersons (N = 8)	Rural Members (N = 79)	Urban Chairpersons (N = 8)	Urban Members (N = 93)	Total Chairpersons (N = 16)	Total Members (N = 172)	Total OEO Funding — Less than $2 Million Chairpersons (N = 12)	Less than $2 Million Members (N = 134)	$2 Million or More Chairpersons (N = 4)	$2 Million or More Members (N = 38)
Review quarterly monitoring reports to be sent to OEO	50	42[a]	50	27[a]	50	34	58	31	25	42
Review applications going to funding agencies	88	39	63	38	75	38	75	37	75	42
Perform and/or review results of venture feasibility studies	75	51	50	46	63	48	75	47	25	53
Review the progress of your CDC in meeting milestones, schedules, and objectives	88	62	75	60	81	60	83	60	75	63
Review reports to be sent to OEO and other funding agencies before they are sent[b]	56	36	60	37	58	37	69	35	33	40

[a] p for chi square test $< .05$.

[b] The N for this variable was 273 for the members, 19 for the chairpersons; 108 members are rural, 165 urban: 193 are from the CDCs, with less than $2 million, 80 from those that have more than $2 million; for chairpersons the breakdowns are 9, 10, 13, and 6 respectively.

Source: The author's 1973 survey of CDC board members and chairpersons.

Prior to examining the two CDC crises, it might be worthwhile to note that board members of business corporations tend to react to these crises in the following ways:

1. They hire a management consultant to perform an overall management audit. If the performance is found to be poor, the problem is often solved by moving the director responsible up to the position of chairperson of the board and by bringing in a new, usually younger, director.

2. The board members who are convinced of impending corporation failure resign, usually for reasons that will not publicly embarrass either the director or the company. Such board members assume that the private communication of their views will have some impact on the remaining members of the board and the executive director. If the corporation is large and listed on one of the major stock exchanges, such resignations are usually signs of impending trouble to the watchdogs from the banking and financial community.

3. The board members can ask or force the chief executive officer to resign. Because this last course is so difficult and so laden with heavy emotion, it is chosen only when the results of bad performance appear to be overwhelming.[12]

Similar options are available for CDC board members. The first option is probably the least likely, since 39 percent of the executive directors have indicated that they might leave the CDC community area if they lost their jobs.[13] Although the CDCs are not listed on the major stock exchanges, board member resignation can be an effective protest so long as CSA and other funding agencies are aware of the reasons for the resignation. Often, if a director is to be removed, the only recourse is to fire him or her or to force the person to resign.

The first case to be reviewed involves the People's Development Corporation (PCD) in Washington, D.C.[14] This corporation began as a subsidiary of another neighborhood corporation, the People's Involvement Corporation (PIC). The executive director of this parent organization chose to leave the parent group to head PDC, in part because he was convinced of the promise of the community economic development movement and in part because the board of directors of the parent organization (PIC) agreed to give him a free hand in his PDC work. PIC chose the majority of the PDC board of directors.

After a couple of years it became evident that the PDC executive director was primarily interested in a crusade against OEO policies, not in implementing board-approved policies for the PDC target area. Over time the executive director's battle with various OEO personnel began to threaten the source of PDC's funds. After much consternation and numerous internal debates, the board voted to remove the offending executive director and to replace him with the then vice-president of PDC. However, by the time these decisions were made, OEO had already decided to terminate PDC.

This is a classic case of a board waiting too long to set criteria for proper management performance, decide collectively that the management was not meeting those criteria, and then remove the manager. Although such delays and the resulting failures are typical even for the boards of major business corporations, such knowledge cannot be much comfort to the PDC community the board was supposed to represent.

The second case, that of the Northeastern Oklahoma Community Development Corporation (NOCDC), is much more complicated, but it is a better example not only of how a CDC executive director is held accountable by the CDC governing board, but also of how the CDC community can hold both the CDC executive director and the board members accountable. The target area of PDC is a predominantly black, inner-city section of Washington, D.C., with a population of about 87,000. In contrast, NOCDC operates in eight northeastern Oklahoma counties occupying about 10,000 square miles and including about 178,000 people. The population is about 70 percent white, 20 percent American Indian (mostly Cherokee and Creek), and 10 percent black.

According to Barry Stein, the author of a detailed case study of the NOCDC crisis, the management crisis began when three or four directors "appeared to some to be actively seeking to change the nature of the corporation away from its basic community focus to something more consistent with their own personal interests."[15] This dissident group first demanded that the NOCDC director of development be fired. When the executive director supported this staff member, the group demanded that both be fired. When the majority of the governing board vetoed these motions, the dissidents successfully moved that a management audit be made by the Washington, D.C., office of OEO. The OEO investigation, however, found no grounds for concluding that the management had performed poorly; it did find, however, that the CDC had not yet established any business ventures in the counties represented by the dissident board members.

One month after this investigation was completed, a series of county shareholders' meetings were scheduled for the purpose of electing new board members from the counties. According to the NOCDC bylaws, one-half of the board (eight members) was to be elected every six months. One of these meetings, in a county represented by one of the dissident board members, had to be canceled because of threats on the lives of the CDC executive director and a candidate opposing the dissident board member. By now the Federal Bureau of Investigation was involved, and news of the internal disruptions within NOCDC was common in the local and regional newspapers. OEO felt it necessary to conduct investigations on the election procedures.

While these investigations were proceeding, 15 percent of the NOCDC shareholders within the counties represented by two of the dissidents signed a recall petition, seeking to remove these two board members from office. These shareholders felt that the executive director, who supported the community-based concept of economic development, should be retained. To make a long story much shorter and simpler than it really was, by November, after the elections, the shareholders had voted in a board of directors who supported the NOCDC staff and the broad goals of community economic development. The new board, despite its passage of a resolution commending the NOCDC employees and expressing the community's appreciation to them, accepted the resignations of five of them, including that of the executive director. The former director of development, over whom the conflict had initially begun, was appointed acting director. This CDC, though less strong than before the conflict, still had the support of OEO and the active support of its shareholders in its target community.

The NOCDC case study appears to demonstrate five things. (1) A few board members will have a very difficult time in attempting to remove an executive director who is popular with other board members and the shareholders. (2) Charges of misdirection of the CDC organization and improper performance must be clearly demonstrated to succeed in removing an executive director. (3) Otherwise uninvolved shareholders can effectively organize to prevent board members from engaging in activities they, the shareholders, do not approve. (4) The crisis created by the conflict will itself tend to produce poor performance, as well as management behavior inimical to favorable development of the CDC, thus producing justification for removal of the executive director even though such justification did not exist at the time of the initial charges. (5) The NOCDC case offers evidence to support the view that control by poor local residents is possible not only over the executive director of the CDC but also over the board members themselves. In this instance "the shareholders rose up and threw the rascals out."[16]

The differences between these two cases deserve some attention. As a subsidiary of PIC, PDC had not developed a constituency of its own among its target area residents, as NOCDC had. It was literally the dependent child of PIC. OEO also played a different role in the two cases. OEO wanted the executive director of PDC removed, but it was at least neutral and at times supportive of the executive director of NOCDC. The PDC offices were within walking distance of the OEO offices, but NOCDC was a long jet flight from Washington, D.C. Hence the NOCDC board members and shareholders were necessarily more independent than the PDC group. It is also worth noting that the CDC that had the higher and more intense levels of board member and shareholder participation during the crisis was the one that weathered the crisis better.

The two cases suggest that CDC governing boards can act during crises involving the executive director, but they also suggest that the very process of resolving a crisis involving a direct confrontation between top management and the board is fraught with extreme danger, threatening the very survival of the CDC, not to memtion its potential for success. Boards would do far better to refine and better utilize the mechanisms available in the operation of the discipline, review, and control function than to permit a severe management crisis to develop.

Exercising Public Leadership

The board members of most business corporations do not have a public leadership function in the way that the members of city councils do. The community development corporation is unique in that it introduces into the business corporation the concept of community control and community involvement. The lay person, usually a resident of a low-income area, is expected to give vitality to the traditional business effort and its experts so that not only the financial, but also the institutional well-being of the poverty-area community will grow. In the past this effort to involve residents of poverty areas in federally sponsored programs has been seen as an attempt to achieve "maximum feasible participation" in a political sense. Presumably, neighborhood residents are better able to articulate policies and programs for the target areas than outsiders are. The criterion for the attainment of "maximum feasible participation" has also been essentially political—the percentage of residents participating in the electoral process.

The community development corporation is not based on this political concept of "maximum feasible participation." The theories underlying the CDC and its relationship to residents are, rather, organizational and business-oriented in nature. They are based on the view that the total configuration of human resources in the community is as vital to economic development as financial and material resources are. These human resources include what Likert describes as "such assets as a firm's human organization, its customer loyalty, shareholder loyalty, its reputation among the financial community, and its reputation in the community in which it has plants and offices."[17] It is largely through the involvement and guidance of the board members that the CDCs hope to build an effective network of these human resources in U.S. poverty environments. The board members become the public leaders not so much of the business aspects of development, which are usually left to the CDC staff and the technical experts, but rather of the human resource development and integration. The board members are to be the previously-missing vital link between business development and the human-resource, institutional aspects of community development. They are to be public leaders like members of city councils, in that they set policies, review existing policies and operations, help form and develop community opinions, and generate support for the CDC programs and goals.

To be effective public leaders in this sense, CDC board members obviously have to interact with and be accountable to individuals and organizations within their communities. At the minimum they must report back to the residents what their CDC is doing and help the residents become involved in those activities. During the Kelly survey, data were collected that permit at least a partial determination of the extent to which CDC board members perform this minimal leadership function. In response to the question, "Do you report board activities back to community residents?" 82 percent of the board members said yes. The highest percentage, however, did not report back to organizations but rather to interested individuals in the area (64 percent). Local neighborhood or block groups (40 percent) and local citizens' associations (29 percent) had the next-highest percentage of members accounting to them. Only 19 percent reported to local business groups, and 18 percent reported to a local community action agency. No variations among the members were found by either geographical location or the amount of funds received from OEO.

In the Kelly survey, 172 of the respondents were also asked to indicate the types of information they gave to the groups to whom they were reporting. For the most part the information reported concerned the CDCs' efforts to produce community economic development. About 58 percent reported progress toward specific goals and about 50 percent reported on new areas of investment, plans and strategies for the future, and benefits the hearers of their reports might expect to get from their CDCs' operations. Another 40 percent said they reported on CDC action taken on loans and ventures. Other items concerning the operational problems of the CDC were reported to the community much less frequently. Only 17 percent reported problems with the board and the CDC staff, while 13 percent reported differences of opinion between the director and the board. About 30 percent gave information on the financial status of the CDC. The only significant differences among the members were that (1) a higher proportion of the members of CDCs receiving $2 million or more from OEO tended to report back to the community on problems with the CDC board and staff (32 percent to 13 percent); and (2) more rural members reported information on CDC action taken in loans and ventures than urban members did.

Slightly different aspects of this public leadership function were tapped by three other questions included in both the Kelly and Abt surveys. Responses to these items revealed that only between one-fourth and one-third of the CDC board members in either 1972 or 1973 performed the specific public leadership tasks of (1) arranging for other individuals or organizations to provide business development or other assistance to the CDC; (2) attending meetings of other organizations as a representative of the CDC, and (3) assisting the CDC in presenting proposals for funding and other support. The chairpersons were much more likely to participate in these activities. In 1973 more than 50 percent of the chairpersons said they had performed these functions.

In sum, the data on reporting back to the community revealed that most board members recognize a public leadership role for themselves as a link between the CDC development efforts and the community. The majority perform that function in some small way at least. In general, however, the vast majority of the CDC board members are not systematically involved in the performance of the more active and more politically oriented public leadership function.

CONCLUSION

The chief purposes of this chapter have been to outline the main functions of a CDC board of directors and to determine whether or not these functions are more comparable with those performed by a traditional governing board of a business corporation or with those performed by more political governing boards, such as those of a city council under the council-manager form of government. The data indicate that the CDC governing board is something of a combination of these two types of boards.

The CDC governing board does not have anywhere near the same level or scope of decision-making powers that a city council has. In this respect the CDC board members perform a function more comparable with that performed by the members of the directorates of business corporations. After the board goals are established and general strategies determined, they approve or disapprove of policies much more than they set them. Most basic business decisions appear to be made by the executive director and the professional staffs. It should be stressed, nonetheless, that they do have control over final policy decisions. The CDC boards, while not dominant over all external and internal power, also do not appear to be rubber stamps.

The chief ways the CDC board members enter the policy-making process appear to be in the initial stages of setting an overall strategy for the CDC and then in the performance of the discipline, review, and control function. The CDC board members also perform the function of acting in crisis stiuations to save their organizations from actual or potential failure. Not as many board members perform these functions as one might wish, but nonetheless the functions are performed in a manner that seems similar to the way those functions are performed by most boards of business corporations and by city councilmen, they also must perform these two functions if their citys' policies are to be effectively implemented.

It was also found that the CDC board members have a public leadership function somewhat like that of city council members. (Most members of business corporation boards do not have this function at all.) The difference in the type of leadership is considerable, however. The city council member must seek to be a leader in choosing among basic policy alternatives in a multitude of areas and informing a particular political constituency. The CDC board member fulfills a leadership role by fostering the development and integration of the human and economic resources in the target area community. The political leader tends to play out his or her role by devising policies for mediating among existing institutions. The CDC board member must also do this, as well as lead in the effort to develop new institutions and new relationships that will further the CDC aims.

What do these findings mean for the reality of community control of CDCs? First, although politics enter into the activities of CDC board members, the decision making they engage in is not as comprehensive as that engaged in by city council members. CDC board members do not have the option of choosing an alternative to the community economic development policy while remaining on the CDC governing board. They can only choose among alternative objectives and means to implement this general policy. Second, because the economic, financial, and political options open to economic developers in low-income, depressed areas are usually restricted sharply by the physical and social environment, even the selection of goals and strategies is somewhat limited. Hence, while the private, nonprofit neighborhood corporation might well be the possible foundation for neighborhood government in the United States, as Kotler argues,[18] it is so only potentially and is still at an embryonic stage. If CDCs are to be more than what they currently are, states will have to charter the CDC as a basic governmental unit.

Finally, because the goals of all the CDCs are within the framework of fostering community-based and community-oriented economic development, it would seem that community control can effectively exist only to the extent that the board members effectively perform their review and control function. It would be in situations where the CDC operating management deviates from the overall goals set by the board and the framework of the community economic development movement that control would be needed. If there is a deviation from established policy or poor management performance, the board (or as in the case of NOCDC, the shareholders) must act. The board members can be in a position to recognize these two situations only if they are performing the discipline, review, and control functions.

NOTES

1. Myles L. Mace, *Directors: Myth and Reality* (Boston: Harvard University Graduate School of Business Administration, 1971), pp. 10-39.

2. Ibid., pp. 26-27.

3. J. M. Juran and J. Keith Louden, in *The Corporate Director* (New York: American Management Association, 1966), pp. 41ff, expand upon Mace's list by including the details of the start-up and self-maintenance functions, but the essential functions are the same as those specified by Mace.

4. Milton Kotler in particular tends to take this position. See his *Neighborhood Government: The Local Foundations of Political Life* (Indianapolis: Bobbs-Merrill, 1969).

5. *Handbook for Councilmen in Council-Manager Cities* (Chicago: International City Managers' Association, 1964).

6. In addition to the *Handbook for Councilmen*, (ibid.), interested readers might wish to look at the more recent and more empirical studies by Charles Levine, *The Job of City Councilman: Devoted Amateur*; Robert Eyestone, *The Threads of Public Policy: A Study in Policy Leadership*; and Heinz Eulau and Kenneth Prewitt, *Patterns of Local Governance: Adaptation, Linkages, and Policies*, all in the Urban Governors Series of the Bobbs-Merrill Company (Indianapolis, Indiana: Bobbs-Merrill).

7. See John C. Weistart, ed., *Community Economic Development* (Dobbs Ferry, N.Y.: Oceana Publications, 1972), p. 28.

8. Rita Mae Kelly, *The Executive Directors of Community Development Corporations: Their Backgrounds, Job Satisfaction, and Use of Work Time* (Cambridge, Mass.: Center for Community Economic Development, 1974).

9. For an analysis of the relationship between city managers and city councils, see Ronald O. Loveridge, *City Managers in Legislative Politics* (Indianapolis: Bobbs-Merrill, 1971).

10. Kotler, *Neighborhood Government*.

11. Rensis Likert's publications in this field are numerous. For a good overview of his ideas and research and a detailed list of the questions he has developed, see his *The Human Organization: Its Management and Value* (New York: McGraw-Hill, 1967) and his *New Patterns of Management* (New York: McGraw-Hill, 1971).

12. For further details, see Mace, *Directors*, pp. 32-42.

13. Kelly, *Executive Directors*.

14. The information for this review of the PDC problems comes from first-hand observation by the author while a consultant at OEO and from conversations with OEO analysts and PDC staff. In the near future a monograph case study of the PDC crisis will be forthcoming from the Center for Community Economic Development, Cambridge, Mass.

15. Barry Stein, *"Throw the Rascals Out": A Case Study of the Northeastern Oklahoma CDC* (Cambridge, Mass.: Center for Community Economic Development, 1973), p. 39. Most of the details on this case come from this source.

16. Ibid., p. 42.

17. Rensis Likert and David G. Bowers, "Organizational Theory and Human Resource Accounting," *American Psychologist*, June 1969, p. 588.

18. Kotler, *Neighborhood Government*.

CHAPTER

5

BOARD CHARACTERISTICS, MEMBER BEHAVIOR, AND THE SUCCESS OF THE COMMUNITY DEVELOPMENT CORPORATION

Up to this point, the discussion has been limited to a basic description of the characteristics, interactions, and functions of the board members. In this chapter I will ask what difference it makes. Does it really matter that the board members differ in their backgrounds and behavior? If it matters, how does it matter? To what extent and in what ways are these characteristics and behaviors or lack of them related to the success of the CDC?

In this chapter specific assumptions about the need and efficacy of community control as a viable concept are also examined. Eleven basic hypotheses, which relate CDC success to factors ranging from the amount of participation in board activities to the degree of accountability to the community, are tested. On the basis of the findings, conclusions are reached about the contribution of community control to community economic development ánd about the activities on which board members can most productively spend their time.

THE SUCCESS RANKINGS

The diversity of objectives and the differing political, geographical, and economic environments make it difficult to develop meaningful success criteria that would be applicable to all CDCs. After three years of effort and over $2 million of labor and time, Abt Associates, the OEO-funded third-party evaluators of the CDCs, had to concede that they had not been able to devise such acceptable criteria of success. The research project upon which this book is based had less than 1 percent of these funds available and about 25 percent of the time. I early recognized the fact that the only possible measure of success for this study would be a measure based on the judgment of knowledgeable experts.

The Judges of the Success of
Community Development Corporations

The judges who ranked the CDCs were OEO staff in the Office of Economic Development in Washington, D.C. They were selected because as a group they had in 1973 the most intimate knowledge of the OEO-funded CDCs in the country, outside of the CDCs themselves, and because their judgments about the success and failure of the CDCs they work with have important practical consequences for the CDCs. Whether the judgment of the OEO personnel is right or wrong by other, "more objective," criteria is often a moot intellectual question, since the judgments of the OEO staff determine whether the CDC will be re-funded, how much money it will receive, what special conditions will be attached to its grants and contracts, and in some instances whether or not the CDC will survive or not. The OEO personnel were also selected because they were accessible and generally willing to cooperate in this endeavor.

Although differences of opinion occurred among the analysts on occasion—the input of at least two OEO staff members went into each—because the data were ultimately grouped into the three categories of least successful (nine CDCs fell here); somewhat successful (eight CDCs fell here); and most successful (eight CDCs fell here), these differences had a minimal affect on the final results. The question used to rank the CDCs by their relative success was "How successful do you think this CDC has been in achieving its goals?" The possible responses ranged on a 20-point, Likert-type scale from generally unsuccessful to generally successful. In the final categorization, the scores of 1-8 were used to define the least successful CDCs; the scores of 9-12 defined the somewhat successful group; and the scores of 13-20 defined the most successful group. (The questionnaire given to the OEO personnel is reproduced in the Appendix.) Due to the refusal of one analyst to complete the assessment form, success rankings were obtained for only 25 of the 26 CDCs included in the Kelly survey; there are 263 members on these 25 boards.

The Criteria Used in Judging Success

As stated earlier, the diversity of goals among the CDCs makes it difficult to devise objective criteria for assessing them and developing a basis for comparative ranking on a so-called success scale. Because of this problem, the OEO personnel were simply asked to judge each CDC on its own merits.

Outside Assessments of the Judges' Accuracy

To obtain an idea of how accurate other knowledgeable experts of the CDCs would consider the OEO assessments of success, a senior staff member of the Center for Community Economic Development was also asked to evaluate the success and failure of the CDCs being studied. He agreed with 88 percent of the judgments. In other words, on only three CDCs was there a difference of opinion. Furthermore, in each case these differences were small; his evaluation would have moved the CDC in question only one category up or down the success scale.

The 263 board members in the Kelly sample were also asked to rate the success of their own CDCs, using the same procedures as the OEO judges. Only 16 declined. The correlation between the board members' ratings and the OEO success ratings was also direct and significant (Kendall Tau C = .12, N = 247, p = .002). On the basis of both of these comparisons, it seems safe to conclude that the success judgments of the OEO staff are sufficiently reasonable and valid for my use here.

FACTORS RELATED TO THE SUCCESS RANKING

Obviously a wide variety of factors contribute to the judgment that a particular CDC is a success or failure. We are concerned with the way in which the OEO judges' perceptions of selected other factors relate to their overall assessments of success or failure. Among the factors examined are the success of the board itself as a policy-setting institution, the extent to which the CDC is judged to have effected community economic development in the target area, and the difficulties in the political and economic environment in which the CDC works.

The data in Table 5.1 show clearly that a very direct and strong relationship exists between the OEO judgment of success of the CDC as an institution and the OEO judgment of success of the board in setting goals, strategies, and policies. While 67 percent of the CDCs with the overall least successful ranking also had their boards ranked as unsuccessful, only 13 percent of the somewhat successful CDCs and none of the most successful CDCs had their boards so ranked. The success rankings the board members gave to their own CDCs were also strongly related to their evaluation of the success of their boards (Tau C = .44, N = 263, p = .00001).

The OEO perception of the CDC's success is also strongly and directly related to its judgment of whether or not the CDC has significantly affected community economic development in its area. While 67 percent of the least successful group of CDCs fell in the "not very significantly" category, none of the somewhat or most successful CDCs did.

Table 5.1 also reveals that there is no direct relationship between the OEO judgment of success of a CDC and the difficulties of the economic environment in the CDC area. This lack of relationship stems largely from the inability of the OEO judges to discriminate among the economic environments, since all are somewhat difficult. A relationship was found to exist between the success

TABLE 5.1

OEO Success Rankings Correlated with
Other OEO Judgments of Community
Development Corporations

	Success Ranking (in percentage)			
Other OEO Judgments	Least (N = 9)	Somewhat (N = 8)	Most (N = 8)	Kendall Tau C[a]
How successful the CDC board has been in setting goals, strategies, and policies				.49[b]
Generally unsuccessful	33	0	0	
Somewhat unsuccessful	33	13	0	
Somewhat successful	33	63	75	
Generally successful	0	25	25	
How much the CDC has affected community economic development in its area				.64[b]
Not very significantly	67	0	0	
Somewhat but not significantly	22	63	38	
Somewhat significantly	11	38	38	
Very significantly	0	0	13	
No data[c]	0	0	13	
How difficult, compared to all other CDCs, the economic environment in the area is				.08
Much more difficult	11	0	13	
Somewhat more difficult	67	75	63	
Somewhat easier	22	25	25	
Much easier	0	0	0	
How difficult, compared to all other CDCs, the political environment in the area is				.21[d]
Much more difficult	33	0	25	
Somewhat more difficult	44	63	38	
Somewhat easier	22	38	25	
Much easier	0	0	13	

[a] The correlations were run using the raw scores from the Likert-type scales against the three success categories. The data are grouped here to present the trends more clearly.

[b] p is less than .001.

[c] For one CDC the OEO judges felt that insufficient data was available to determine yet whether or not community economic development in the area had been affected.

[d] p = .066.

Source: The 1973 survey of community economic development monitors in the OEO, conducted by the author.

TABLE 5.2

OEO Perception and Success Ranking of CDC Goals
(in percent)

	Success Ranking		
	Least (N = 9)	Somewhat (N = 8)	Most (N = 8)
Creating jobs	67	75	38
Developing profitable businesses	89	63	25
Reducing unemployment	0	25	38
Providing manpower training and development	11	0	25
Providing opportunities for local individual ownership of business and property	33	0	38
Providing opportunities for community-controlled ownership of business and property	22	63	50
Reducing community deterioration (developing land, resources, and property)	22	13	38
Reducing community dependence on outsiders	11	38	25
Increasing incomes of those already employed	11	25	0
Reducing number of people leaving the area	0	0	25
Getting outside institutions to aid in community development	33	0	0

Source: The 1973 survey of community economic development monitors in the OEO, conducted by the author.

rankings and the OEO assessment of the difficulty of the CDC's political environment. The easier the political environment, the higher the success ranking; only CDCs in the most successful group had a "much easier" political environment. In effect, Table 5.1 suggest that an obviously easier political environment may contribute to success but that an obviously difficult one does not necessarily mean failure.

The OEO judges of CDC success were also asked to specify the three most important objectives that, in their opinion, the CDC had set for itself. The comparison of the OEO success judgment with the OEO perception of the CDC's chief goals (see Table 5.2) shows that when OEO personnel perceive the goals of developing profitable businesses and getting outside institutions to aid in community development as being among the top three for the CDC, they are also more likely to judge that CDC a failure. When OEO perceives the objectives as reducing unemployment, providing manpower training and development, providing opportunities for community-controlled ownership of businesses and property, and reducing the number of people leaving the area, they are more likely to judge the CDC a success. The latter objectives are more directly and uniquely related to the enabling legislation for the CDC program than are those of developing profitable businesses and getting outside institutions to aid community development.

Characteristics Related to Success of Community Development Corporations

Throughout this study we have been examining the impact the rural-urban location of the CDC and the amount of money received from OEO have on the survey findings. As Table 5.3 shows, the comparison of the geographical location of the CDC with the success rating revealed no sharp differences. Nor were major differences found when the CDCs were compared in terms of whether they had first received OEO funds before 1969 or in 1970 or later. One might expect that those funded over the longest period of time would be considered the most successful by OEO, but this is not true. (See Table 5.3.)

TABLE 5.3

Location and Age and OEO Success Ranking
(in percent)

	Success Ranking		
CDC Characteristic	Least (N = 9)	Somewhat (N = 8)	Most (N = 8)
Geographical location			
Rural	44	50	38
Urban	56	50	63
Year CDC first received OEO funds			
1969 or earlier	33	25	38
1970 or later	67	75	63

Source: The 1973 survey of community economic development monitors in the OEO, conducted by the author.

TABLE 5.4

Kendall Tau C Rank Order Correlations of OEO Rankings and CDC Characteristics

CDC Characteristic	Success Ranking (in percent)			
	Least (N = 9)	Somewhat (N = 8)	Most (N = 8)	Kendall Tau C
Amount of money received from OEO				.29[a]
Less than $2 million	78	75	38	
$2 million or more	22	25	63	
Number of executive directors				−.08
2 or fewer	67	88	100	
3 or more	33	13	0	
Turnover rate of executive directors[b]				−.04
33 or less	33	87	25	
34 to 66	44	13	63	
67 to 100	22	0	13	
Number of board chairmen				−.05
2 or fewer	78	87	87	
3 or more	22	13	13	
Turnover rate of board chairmen[b]				.02
33 or less	11	50	13	
34 to 66	78	38	63	
67 to 100	11	13	25	

[a] $p < .02$.

[b] The basic information on the turnover of directors and chairpersons was obtained from the Office of Economic Opportunity analyst responsible for the particular CDC. The number of directors of the CDC was divided by the number of years the CDC received funds from OEO, which in almost all instances began with the birth of the CDC. To get a standard turnover rate, the resulting fraction was multiplied by 100. If the CDC had a new director every year, the turnover rate would be 100.

Note: The raw data were used for these correlations. The groupings here are simply to give a clearer picture to the non-statistically-oriented person of the meaning behind the correlation.

Source: The 1973 survey of community economic development monitors in the OEO, conducted by the author.

A difference was found, however, when the amounts of funds received from OEO was examined. While close to two-thirds of the most successful CDCs had received $2 million or more from OEO since their inception, only about one-fourth of the somewhat and least successful CDCs had received that much. (See Table 5.4.) Such a relationship would be expected, in part because initial successes bring in more money. The more money the CDC has, the more leverage it has, thus increasing the odds it will have the needed resources to attain its goals.

An important characteristic of the CDC is said to be the stability of its key leaders. Hence the success ratings were compared with both the actual number of directors and chairpersons the CDCs had had in their existence and also with their turnover rates. This latter variable corrects for variations in the length of time the CDC has existed, producing comparability in the raw data on the number of people in key positions. The results in Table 5.4 show that no significant relationship was found between the success of the CDC and the turnover of the directors. In terms of the actual number of directors the CDCs have had, however, 100 percent of the most successful CDCs have had two directors or fewer, while 88 percent of the somewhat successful CDCs and 67 percent of the least successful CDCs had had 2 or fewer directors. In other words, although one might think, on the basis of the raw numbers of directors that the CDCs have had, that the probability of a CDC being successful would be strongly related to the continuity and stability of the leader in the position of executive director, the statistical analyses, particularly on the turnover rate, do not support this supposition. The data on the board chairpersons also showed no significant differences among the CDCs in terms of the stability of the chairpersons and the CDCs' success.

In the Kelly survey, the board members were asked how long they had held these positions. As Table 5.5 shows, the stability and continuity of the

TABLE 5.5

Success and Length of Time as Board Members (in percent)

Length of Time as a Board Member	Least Successful (N = 79)	Somewhat Successful (N = 94)	Most Successful (N = 73)
12 months or less	41	39	26
13-24 months	30	29	22
25-36 months	17	19	23
37 months or more	13	13	29

Note: Kendall Tau C = .149; p < .0003.

Source: The author's 1973 surveys of CDC board members and of the OEO community economic development monitors.

CDC board members seem to be critical to CDC success. The longer the board members have been members, the greater the likelihood that their CDCs will be successful. While 52 percent of the members of the most successful CDCs have been members 25 months or more, only 30 percent of the members of the least successful CDCs have been. Because in the past OEO has set as a special condition the requirement that new board members be elected after three years, it is worth noting that the members of the most successful CDCs were more than twice as often members for three years or more than were the members of either the least or the somewhat successful CDCs. The Community Services Administration (CSA) might wish to reconsider this position in light of these findings.

Board Members' Background Characteristics and Success of the Community Development Corporation

Table 5.6 reveals that of the five background variables examined—race, sex, education, area of academic specialization, and age—only race was significantly related to the success of the CDC. Among the least successful CDCs, 68 percent of the board members are black, 7 percent from some other minority group, and 8 percent white. Among the most successful CDCs, 41 percent of the members are white, 44 percent black, and 12 percent from some other minority group. Because the OEO staff making these judgments is about 50 percent black, it is doubtful that the variation found here is the result of racial prejudice. The situations of the predominately black CDCs are usually quite different from those of the predominately white ones. The black CDCs tend to be in urban areas with difficult political environments, while the white CDCs tend to be in rural areas with less hostile political environments. As the data in Table 5.1 revealed, the OEO judgment of the CDC's success was related to this factor. The no-answer category in this question, as well as the others on this table, basically comes from two CDCs. Both of these CDCs received "least successful" ratings and both CDC board are about 75 percent black. Hence the inclusion of that information should have made the differences found here even more sharp than they are now.

It is somewhat surprising that the education and areas of academic specialization of the board members are not related with the success of the CDC. On occasion, OEO and CSA personnel have objected strongly to the lack of business and economic training of CDC staff and board members, under the assumption that those areas of specialization make a meaningful difference. The data here indicate that such academic training does not distinguish the board members of the more successful CDCs from those of the less successful CDCs.

Because of the common suspicion that people with college or advanced educations will be more effective in special postions on CDC boards, the educational data were reexamined, controlling for the special positions held on the board. As Table 5.7 shows, no statistically significant differences were found.

TABLE 5.6

Success and Board Members' Background Characteristics
(in percent)

	Least Successful (N = 90)	Somewhat Successful (N = 100)	Most Successful (N = 73)
Race			
Black	68	27	44
Other minority	7	34	12
White	8	35	41
No answer	18	4	3
	$x^2 = 58.79$ 4 df p < .001		
Sex			
Female	26	20	33
Male	60	78	64
No answer	14	2	3
	$x^2 = 4.12$ 2 df p = NS		
Education			
High school or less	33	38	43
College or some advanced higher education	28	35	34
Graduate work, master's degrees, and doctorates	24	25	23
No answer	14	2	0
	$x^2 = .71$ 2 df p = NS		
Area of specialization			
Business economics	20	19	24
All other	30	39	33
No answer	50	42	42
	$x^2 = 1.17$ 2 df p = NS		
Age			
34 or less	18	18	11
35 to 49	29	48	41
50 or more	37	31	44
No answer	17	3	4
	$x^2 = 6.796$ 4 df p = NS		

Source: The author's 1973 surveys of CDC board members and of the OEO community economic development monitors.

Although 16 percent more of the board members holding special positions in most successful CDCs had college education or some advanced training after high school, compared with the least successful group's board members (49 percent to 33 percent), 10 percent more of the most successful CDCs' members holding special positions had high school or less education as well

TABLE 5.7

Success and Participation of Members:
Controlled by Education
(in percent)

Level of Education	Least Successful (N = 90)	Somewhat Successful (N = 100)	Most Successful (N = 73)
High school or less			
No special position	14	21	11
Special position	19	17	29
College or some advanced higher education			
No special position	19	23	11
Special position	33	37	49
No data	14	2	0

Note: x^2 = 10.5 6 df p = NS

Source: The author's 1973 surveys of the CDC board members and of the OEO community economic development monitors.

(29 percent to 19 percent). The critical difference, therefore, does not seem to be education, but rather the amount of participation by the members regardless of education. (See the discussion of the first hypothesis below for further analyses of this issue.)

Board Members' Prior Work Experience
and CDC Success

In Chapter 3 it was pointed out that the background work experiences of the members and CDC boards of directors are not typical of those of most advisors to business and economic development institutions. Because they are different and because what is being tried in the community economic development area is new, it is important to inquire which prior work experiences seem most helpful to board members in their efforts to guide the CDCs to success. The data in Table 5.8 reveal that the CDC's success rating is higher when the board members indicate they have worked in some capacity with a local business, a local business development group, or a neighborhood association. The CDC's success rating is lower when the board members indicate that they have experience working with schools or universities; churches; or a federal, local, or state government agency. The data on the experience of the board members as advisors or trustees or members of other institutions' boards of directors showed that CDCs with more board members that had such prior policy-making experience on the directorates of local businesses, industries, churches, and community agencies were the most likely to be successful.

On the basis of these findings it appears that on-the-job experience is primarily helpful to board members in the business-related work areas. Having large numbers of board members previously or currently employed in the non-profit-making and non-profit-oriented institutions of schools or universities, churches, and governmental agencies appears to be a handicap to the CDC. Prior experience as a board member, however, seems to enhance the CDC's chances of

TABLE 5.8

Prior Work Experience and Success:
Kendall Tau C Correlations

Prior Work Experience	As Employee (n = 254)	As Board Member, Advisor, or Trustee	n
Banking/lending institution	−.04	.15	33
School/university	−.06[a]	−.003	48
Local business	.07[b]	.16[b]	62
Industry	.03	.32[b]	29
Church	−.12[b]	.10[a]	104
Business development group (chamber of commerce)	.06[a]	.12	50
Neighborhood association (such as local coop, gangs)	.08[b]	.07	105
Local political body (such as local citizen's association)	−.01	.03	88
Community agency (such as CAP or CEP)	−.01	.16[b]	105
Government agency (federal, state, or local)	−.07[a]	.11	58
Union	−.02	.01	37

Note: These correlations assume that the work experience variable is on an ordinal scale, with the persons having had the work experience ranking higher than those who have not had it. This assumption permits the testing of the following hypothesis; the greater the experience of board members in these particular work areas, the greater the success ranking. The "no" responses were scored as 1, the "yes" responses as 2.

[a] $p < .10$ but $> .05$.
[b] $p < .05$.

Source: The author's 1973 surveys of the CDC board members and of the OEO community economic development monitors.

success, regardless of the profit or nonprofit status of the institution or its economic or noneconomic nature.

Board Member Behavior and CDC Success

One need not be a critical observer to note that collective ownership can exist without community control. In other words, there should be a meaningful difference between actual control over the policies of an institution and simple ownership of a part of it. By and large, the practical meaning and processes of community control have escaped serious empirical analysis. While its virtues and vices are expounded upon almost daily, the nitty-gritty reality eludes us. Although it would be presumptuous to assume that the total reality of community control will be meaningfully presented here, it is hoped that a testing of the hypotheses presented below will advance our knowledge about community control and simultaneously provide useful insights for the CDC board members, executive directors, and other interested parties.

Hypothesis 1. The greater the participation of the board members in board activities, the greater the success of the CDC. In seeking to test this hypothesis empirically, several different indicators were used. First, it was assumed that if the hypothesis is correct, then the data will show that a larger proportion of the members of the most successful CDCs participate more in some special capacity, as committee chairpersons, officers, or members, than do the members

TABLE 5.9

Relationship between Board Member Participation and Success Ranking
(in percent)

Level of Member Participation	Success Ranking		
	Least (N = 90)	Somewhat (N = 100)	Most (N = 73)
No special participation	37	44	19
Committee member	28	28	37
Committee chairperson or officer	35	27	44

Note: x^2 = 12.56; 4 degrees of freedom; p < .01; Kendall Tau C = .10; p < .008.
Source: The author's 1973 surveys of the CDC board members and of the OEO community economic monitors.

TABLE 5.10

Attendance at CDC-Related Meetings and Success
(in percent)

	Success Ranking		
Number of Meetings attended in Past Three Months	Least (N = 90)	Somewhat (N = 100)	Most (N = 73)
Two or fewer	24	32	16
Three	34	50	48
Four or more	34	35	29
No data	7	4	7

Note: x^2 = 15.37; 4 degrees of freedom; p <.004; Kendall Tau C = – .003; p = NS.
Source: The author's 1973 surveys of the CDC board members and of the OEO community economic development monitors.

of the less successful CDCs. In other words, in the least successful CDCs, fewer members will be doing the bulk of the work.

The data in Table 5.9 on special positions reveal that this assumption is, in fact, correct. Only 19 percent of the members of the most successful CDCs have no special positions. Although it is possible that this finding is the result of some bias in the sample, no evidence that I have been able to detect indicates it is. As was pointed out in Chapter 4, no differences on this variable were found among the members in terms of rural-urban location or the amount of funds the CDCs had received from OEO.

Second, if the hypothesis is correct, more meetings will have been attended in the previous three months by the board members of the successful CDCs. As expected, a smaller percentage of the members of the most successful CDCs (16 percent) attended two or fewer of the CDC meetings than the members of the least successful CDCs (24 percent), but the relationship between attendance at meetings and the success ranking is not linear. (See Table 5.10.) The members of the somewhat successful CDCs attended fewer meetings on the average than even the members of the least successful CDCs. It appears that attendance at meetings is not so clearly related to success as additional participation on committees is.

Hypothesis 2. The greater the involvement of the board of directors with CDC staff and activities, the greater the success of the CDC. To test this hypothesis and several others presented below, the overall scores of the board members on a series of items on the "Profile of the Board and the CDC" presented in Chapter 4 were correlated with the success ranking, using the Kendall Tau C rank-order correlation. As the results in Table 5.11 show, no statistically significant correlation was found. Hence, one has to reject this hypothesis. The success

TABLE 5.11

Indices of Organizational Characteristics and Success Ranking: Kendall Tau C Correlations

Index	Board Weak			Board Strong	Kendall Tau C
Leadership Interaction					
1. How free do the CDC staff members feel to talk to the board members about their jobs?	Not very free	Slightly free	Quite free	Very free	-.055[a]
2. How free does the executive director feel to talk to board members about his job?	Not very free	Slightly free	Quite free	Very free	-.011 } -.0006
3. Are staff members' ideas sought and used in making board decisions?	Not very often	Sometimes	Usually	Almost always	.074[b]
Motivational forces					
4. In trying to increase involvement and output of other board members and of the CDC staff, what do board members stress primarily?	Economic security	Status and achievement	New experiences, pride	CDC and community needs	.100[b] } .017
5. Who on the board feels the most responsibility for achieving the CDC's goals?	Mostly the director, not the board	Mostly the board chairperson	Chairperson and few others	Almost all	-.004
Communication processes					
6. How much do you talk with CDC staff (including the director) about achieving CDC goals?	Very little	Little	Quite a bit	A great deal	.058[a]
7. How accurate is the communication from the staff to the board?	Often wrong	Sometimes wrong	Usually accurate	Accurate	-.107[b] } -.037
8. How well does the board know the problems faced by the staff?	Very little	Some	Knows quite well	Very well	-.059[a]

124

Decision-making processes

	Mostly the director, not the board	Board chairperson	Chairperson and a few other members	Almost all the board	
9. Who on the board really makes the most important policy decisions?					.012
10. Who on the board has the technical and professional knowledge that is generally used in decision making excluding consultants?	CDC staff not the board	Board Chairperson	Chairperson and a few others	Almost all the board	−.099[b] ⎱ −.07[b]
11. Does the way your board makes decisions make the board members want to work harder to achieve CDC goals?	Not usually	Yes, a little	Yes, some	Yes, a lot	.031

Goal-setting processes

12. How are your CDC's goals established?	Orders by board	Orders by board and director	Orders after talks with staff	By group action of all	−.027
13. How much do staff (including the director) resist board-set goals and decisions?	Very great deal	Quite a bit	Some	Very little	.024 ⎱ −.006

Review and control processes

14. How concentrated are the review and control functions for evaluating employee and venture performance?	In hands of director only	Director, board chairperson only	Director, chairperson, and a few others	Director, plus almost all of board	−.013
15. What does the CDC board use cost, productivity, and other control data for?	Nothing — Policing staff	Reward and punishment	Reward Some self-guidance	Problem solving	−.021 ⎱ −.022
Overall Score					+ −.046

[a] p for Kendall Tau C is less than .10, but greater than .05.
[b] p for Kendall Tau C is less than .05.

Source: The author's 1973 surveys of the CDC board members and of the OEO community economic development monitors. The general form for this profile was modified from Form S in Appendix II in *The Human Organization: Its Management and Value* by Rensis Likert. Copyright 1967 by McGraw-Hill Book Company and the author. Used by permission of McGraw-Hill Book Company and the author. No further use, reproduction, or distribution of Form S is authorized.

ranking of the CDC does not increase directly with the amount of board involvement in CDC staff and activities.

Hypothesis 3. The greater the interaction of the CDC leadership, (Board members, staff, and executive director), the greater the success ranking. The profile of the board and the CDC included three items on the interaction of the CDC leadership. The higher the score, the greater the interaction. If higher amounts of interaction are in fact related to CDC success, then we should find that the combined index for these items (see Table 5.11) will be positively correlated with the success ranking. Such is not the case, however. Again, the hypothesis must be rejected. Increased interaction in general is not directly related to CDC success.

An examination of the specific items composing the index reveals, nonetheless, that some types of interaction of the board with the staff are more positive in producing success and some more negative. Item 1 in Table 5.11 shows a negative correlation, indicating that the freer the staff members feel to talk to board members about their jobs, the lower the success ranking. This finding might mean that greater freedom on the part of staff to go to the board members is related to a weakened position for the director. Interference on the part of board members in line-staff relationships could undercut the director, upsetting the director's efforts at implementation of goals.

Item 3, which concerns seeking and using staff members' ideas in the making of board decisions, shows a strong positive correlation with the CDC's success. The more frequently the staff members' ideas are sought and used in decision making, the greater the success ranking. This latter finding suggests that reliance upon the technical and professional competence of the CDC staff is wise.

Hypothesis 4. The more the board members are motivated by community and CDC needs and not personal needs and status, the greater the likelihood of CDC success. Item 4 in the profile was used to test this hypothesis. The strong positive correlation reveals that it is supported by the data. The success ranking does rise directly as board members perceive themselves and the staff as being motivated by community rather than personal needs.

Hypothesis 5. The more everyone on the board feels responsibility for achieving CDC goals, the greater the likelihood of success. Item 5 was used to test this hypothesis. It was not supported. This finding might be due to the fact that the feeling of responsibility was equally high for all board members regardless of the success ranking of their CDCs. The critical factor, as will be indicated during the discussion of hypothesis 10, is not how many feel responsibility but how many actually do something to demonstrate that responsibility.

Hypothesis 6. The better the communication processes between the CDC staff and CDC board, the greater the likelihood of success. The overall index of the communication processes produced no significant correlation with the success rankings of the CDCs. (See Table 5.11.) Hence the hypothesis must be rejected.

A more detailed examination of the items composing the index explains this seemingly unexpected result. First, in item 6, which concerns the extent to which the board members talk to CDC staff, including the director, about achieving CDC goals, a positive correlation exists. That is, the more the board members engage in such conversations, the more likely probable success will occur. On items 7 and 8, however, negative correlations exist. The negative relationship for item 7 is particularly strong. The question asked is, "How accurate is the communication from the staff to the board?" If one were extremely literal, one could conclude that the less accurate the communication from the staff to the board, the greater the probability of success. It is quite doubtful, though, that that is the actual meaning of this inverse relationship. The finding is more correctly interpreted to mean that when the board members are more critical of the accuracy and substance of the communications being presented to them by their staffs there is a greater probability of success. (See more on this in the discussion of hypothesis 10.)

The inverse correlation on item 8 shows that the success ranking of the CDC is higher when the board members know the problems of the staff less well. Again the findings suggest that success will be greatest when the board is less, not more, intimately involved with the staff.

Hypothesis 7. The greater the board of directors' involvement in decision making in general, the greater the success of the CDC. Included among the questions relating to the profile of the board and the CDC were items concerning the decision-making processes. One such item directly asked, "Who on the board really makes the most important policy decisions?" No statistically significant difference was found here between indication of involvement in decision making and the CDC's success ranking. Table 5.11 does show, however, that a strong connection exists to the responses to the question, "Who on the board has the technical and professional knowledge that is generally used in decision making (excluding consultants)?" Contrary to what one might expect on the basis of the hypothesis, the relationship is inverse. When the score is lower, that is, when the technical knowledge is perceived to reside with the CDC staff or a few board members, the likelihood of a higher success ranking is greater.

On the basis of these findings, it would appear that the hypothesis as stated is incorrect. Greater involvement of the board in decision making in general is not directly related to the CDCs' success. Further, it would seem that success is actually greater when the board members explicitly recognize their limitations in the technical and professional areas and rely on those who do have that knowledge.

Because many people argue that decision making and policy making are supposed to be the critical roles of the board, it was decided to test more specific hypotheses about the relationship with CDC success of certain types of decision making by the board.

Hypothesis 8. When the most important decisions of a year concern the setting of specific goals and policies of operation, the CDC is more likely to be successful than when the board is concerned either with broader, long-term strategy or structural-functional problems of implementation and operation. One underlying assumption of this hypothesis is that when boards are too abstract they give insufficient guidance to their organizations. In effect, a board concerned with long-term goals would be that of an organization either just starting up or operating without any effective community control. Another underlying assumption is that when board members are concerned with the structural-functional problems of their CDCs, either they are having internal administrative problems or the members are meddling in affairs best left to the executive director.

The data used to test this hypothesis are the responses of the board members to the question, "What are the most important decisions the board has made in the past year?" As Table 5.12 shows, the hypothesis is generally supported by the data. A strong difference exists between the least and most successful CDCs, in that a much greater proportion of the more successful CDCs' members choose the response "making 'go, no go' decisions about specific ventures, loans, and investments" than did the members of the least successful CDCs. This would support the hypothesis. No significant relationship exists between any of the first three types of decisions listed in Table 5.12 and success. All three of these are at a more abstract level.

The findings on the remaining types of decisions, all of which involve structural-functional problems, also tend to support the hypothesis. No significant difference between success and the last three variables exists. When the CDC members indicated that one of the three most important decisions of the past year was the choosing of the executive director, however, a strong, inverse relationship is revealed; that is, there is less likelihood that the CDC will be successful. A significant difference also appeared when the board members indicated that one of the three most important decisions was the changing of the executive director. Here the meaning of the difference is less clear, however, since both the least and the most successful CDCs were the ones having the highest proportion of members saying that this had been one of the three most important decisions of the past year.

Hypothesis 9. Board member participation in policy-related review and control functions is more critical to CDC success than board member participation in the public leadership functions of mediating between the CDC and other

TABLE 5.12

Most Important Decisions of Past Year and Success

Decision	Success Ranking (percent selecting item as one of three)		
	Least (N = 84)	Somewhat (N = 98)	Most (N = 71)
Establishing an overall strategy	48	50	54
Setting goals for the year	44	52	52
Determining the general kinds of businesses to invest in	50	59	44
Making "go, no go" decisions about specific ventures, loans, and investments	30*	51*	52*
Choosing the executive director	30*	6*	16*
Changing the executive director	21*	3*	18*
Requesting more funds and/or time from a funding source such as OEO	31	33	37
Investing in a MESBIC	6	9	1
Establishing or revising personnel policies and procedures	25	27	25

*p for x^2, 2 degrees of freedom. Comparing these responses indicates that the items were selected among the top three decisions, with the proportion saying the items were not selected in each success rank less than .005.

Source: The author's surveys of the CDC board members and of the OEO community economic development monitors.

organizations and acting as the CDC's representative, or in actually engaging in the implementation of CDC policies.

Hypothesis 10. The greater the involvement of the board in the review and control functions, the greater the success of the CDC. The above two hypotheses are presented together because they are related and because both are tested by the data in Table 5.13. Hypothesis 9 involves the examination of the relative importance of different functions that the board members actually do perform. If the hypothesis is correct, then there should be a statistically significant relationship between the success of the CDC and the review and control functions and no statistically significant differences between success and the other functions. In fact, the results show precisely this. The functions of reviewing venture feasibility studies, quarterly monitoring reports to be sent to OEO,

TABLE 5.13

Performance of Specific Functions and Success:
Kendall Tau C Correlations for 152 Members

Function	Kendall Tau C
Provide technical advice to director[a] and staff	.055
Perform and/or review results of venture feasibility studies	.135[b]
Arrange for other individuals or organizations to provide business development or other assistance to the CDC	.019
Attend meetings of other organizations as a representative of the CDC	.010
Assist the CDC in presenting proposals for funding and other support	.025
Review quarterly monitoring reports to be sent to OEO	.142[b]
Review applications going to funding agencies[a]	.217[b]
Review the progress of the CDC in meeting milestones, schedules, and objectives	.204[b]
Planning overall strategy and goals for the CDC 5, 10, and 15 years in future[a]	.149[b]
Do you review reports before sent to OEO?[c]	.061[d]

[a] An additional person chose not to answer this specific item; thus N = 151.

[b] p (significance level) for the Kendall Tau C is less than .005.

[c] This item was included in all the questionnaires. The N upon which the correlation is based = 234, with 29 not answering (out of the possible 263 board members in the 25 CDCs ranked).

[d] p = .082

Note: These correlations assume that the performance of the board members' functions can be placed on an ordinal scale, with a 1 being given to nonperformance and a 2 being given to the performance of the function. This scale is then correlated to the success ranks of the CDCs from which the members come. The hypothesis being tested, then, is that the higher the rank the member receives on the performance variable, the higher will be the success ranking for the CDC. The question concerning the performance of these functions was included in only 172 of the questionnaires. The n of 152 stems from the fact that 20 persons chose not to answer the questions at all.

Source: The author's 1973 survey of the CDC board members and the OEO community economic development monitors.

and applications to funding agencies and assessing the progress of the CDC in meeting milestones, schedules, and objectives are all directly and significantly related to the success rankings the CDCs received. Of four other functions connected with advising the staff, mediating between the CDC and other organizations, acting as the CDC's representatives, or engaging in implementation policies, not one is significantly related to CDC success. It is worth noting that planning the overall strategy and goals for the CDC five, ten, and fifteen years in the future is also directly related to the success of the CDC.

Hypothesis 10 concerns the issue of whether or not it makes any difference how many on the baord of directors perform this review and control function. Does it matter if a few, a self-selected elite perform this review and control function, or does it really make a difference if a greater proportion of board members participate? This issue is of great importance for the community control concept. If the active participation of board members does not matter, then community control is a mythology, a meaningless ideological trick. The results in Table 5.13, however, show that participation does matter. In every instance in which the review and control and planning functions are examined, there is a strong, direct, positive relationship between board member participation and the success of the CDC.

A question related to the performance of the review and control function, particularly with regard to reviewing reports, is whether it matters when the function is performed before or after the reports are submitted to outside funding agencies? A strong suspicion exists among the federal monitors that several boards are not reviewing them before they are submitted by the directors. The data from the Kelly survey substantiate that suspicion: 58 percent of the board members do not review the reports before they are sent, don't review them at all, or don't know whether they review them before or after they are sent. With regard to the question of whether it matters when they are reviewed, the statistical tests suggest that there is a greater probability that the CDC will be successful if the reports are reviewed by the board members prior to being submitted to the funding agencies. (See Table 5.13.)

Several of the items included in the profile of the board and the CDC also concerned this review and control function. No significant differences were found in the profile data that would distinguish the more successful from the less successful CDCs on either the individual items (see Table 5.11) or the total index for board participation in the review and control process.

At first glance this lack of significance in the profile data appears to contradict the findings from the functions data. It might be, however, that the wording of the question evoked the phrase "technical and professional knowledge" of an earlier question in the profile. As was already noted, success is related to having board members defer to those with knowledge. Because approximately 40 percent of the board members have high school educations or less and are probably not experienced in accounting, personnel performance evaluation, and so on, the results here probably relate more to this variation than contradict the finding that greater participation is beneficial to CDC success.

The issue would be the point at which the participation begins. The actual evaluation of the employees' and ventures' performances might well be done by the CDC director and staff with the assistance of certain board members or committees, but the review of the results of these evaluations would be conducted by the board at large. The data indicate that this latter type of review is critical to the CDC's success, but there is no relationship between the status of those who actually perform the evaluations and CDC success.

The data on the communication processes within the CDC also show the importance of the broad review and control functions of the board of directors. The more critical the board members were of the accuracy of the information received, the higher the success ranking of their CDCs. Again, the evidence indicates that the more questioning and critical the board members are of their staff (within the positive context of reviewing activities in relation to CDC goals), the more likely it is that their CDC will be successful. It should also be noted that the correlation between item 6 in Table 5.11 (talking with the director and CDC staff about achieving the CDC goals) and success is positive. That is, the more encouragement and discusssion about goal achievement, the greater the success ranking is likely to be. Hence it is conscientious performance of the review and control function that requires a critical view of the accuracy of the information received; the critical review does not extend to or imply that greater success will be obtained by general or negative criticisms of the director and staff. To the contrary, the data suggest that board efforts to motivate and encourage the staff within a positive framework are also important to CDC success.

Hypothesis 11. The greater the accountability to the target area community, the greater the likelihood of success. As was pointed out in the previous chapter, OEO (CSA) places considerable emphasis upon the necessity that the CDC board of directors be "accountable" to the target area community. Here we wish to examine some aspects of that accountability to see what, if any, connection there might be between that accountability and CDC success.

For the main measure of accountability, the items are used that concern whether or not the board members report back to their communities and to whom. Although these behaviors can be indicators of public leadership as described in Chapter 4, they also are ways of accounting to constituents. Again, to test the hypothesis that the greater the accountability, the greater the success, the reporting-back data are placed on an ordinal scale, with reporting back treated as ranking higher than not reporting back. The data in Table 5.14 show that the hypothesis is supported. The higher the CDC board member ranks on reporting back to the community, the higher the ranking of the CDC on the success scale.

Using similar statistical procedures, an effort was made to determine whether success is related to accountability to particular groups. The results in Table 5.14 show that it is. The higher the members score on reporting back to a local community action agency and to local neighborhood or block groups, the greater the success ranking. Conversely, the lower the members score on reporting back to local business groups and to interested individuals, the higher the success ranking. Apparently, being accountable to local business groups

TABLE 5.14

Correlations between Reporting to the Community and Success

To Whom Reporting	Kendall Tau C	N	P
Community residents in general	.065	261	.059
A local CAP agency	.096	215	.017
Area association	.003	216	.475
Local neighborhood or block groups	.065	216	.077
Local business groups	−.068	216	.067
Interested individuals in area	−.136	216	.001

Source: The author's 1973 surveys of the CDC board members and of the community economic development monitors.

and private individuals adversely affects the success of a community development corporation. Perhaps the data here reflect problems of conflict of interest.

Pursuing this matter of accountability further, the data on the type of information were also examined to see whether the members of the more successful CDCs differed from those of the less successful CDCs in terms of what they report back to residents. It was found that the members of the more successful CDCs tend to report information on new areas of investment and on plans and strategies for the future significantly more than the members of the least successful CDCs.

In conclusion, it would seem that the greater the accountability to target area residents, the greater the likelihood of success. It also seems that it matters to whom the members are accountable. Accounting to private businesses and individuals appears to affect CDC success adversely, while being accountable to organizations representing the community as a whole affects success positively.

CONCLUSION

The analyses in this chapter clearly show that the characteristics of the CDC board members and member behavior and the success of the CDC are strongly related. CDC success as a whole is directly related to the success of the board in setting goals, strategies, and policies. Success is also related to the goals the board sets for the CDC and the extent to which the board members work with other board members and the staff to attain those goals. While participation in board activities at high levels seems to enhance the chances of

CDC success, higher levels of involvement with the CDC staff and all CDC activities by board members does not seeem to be related positively to success.

The data suggest that the role of the board members is vital to success, but also that their role must be carefully defined and that a careful distinction needs to be maintained between the power, prerogatives, and responsibilities of the board members and of the executive director if success is to be achieved. The most important functions the board members fulfill are the review and control functions at a general policy level. Community control of community economic development in the sense of policy setting and review of progress is essential to success, but apparently so is a hands-off policy on the part of the board members in most decision making at the implementation level. There is a strong connection between CDC success and the willingness of the board members to defer to experts in technical and professional matters.

6

COMMUNITY ECONOMIC DEVELOPMENT: ITS SIGNIFICANCE FOR POOR PEOPLE AND FOR PARTICIPATORY DEMOCRACY AND COMMUNITY CONTROL

CDCs are viewed by many observers as a means of revitalizing the economic life of low-income areas. The community economic development movement is seen as a way of making an economic development ethnic compatible with the existing beliefs of poor people. The CDCs are also viewed as a new form of grassroots, participatory democracy and as a true-life example of community control over a vital area of human activity. At this point it is necessary to assess the extent to which the data presented in this study support these assertions and the assumption that citizen participation has a positive effect on the CDCs' success.

THE SIGNIFICANCE OF COMMUNITY ECONOMIC DEVELOPMENT FOR POOR PEOPLE

An Alternative Philosophy for Economic Development

Most Americans have been imbued with the essential elements of the capitalist ideology. As was pointed out in Chapter 2, the community economic development movement is only partly based on the capitalist outlook. Entrepreneurship and profitability are stressed, but the basic assumptions about the nature of human beings and their relationship to their communities differ from the traditional capitalist ideology.

Capitalism assumes that the fulfillment of human needs is primarily an individual rather than a community concern.[1] It also assumes that human beings are acquisitive and competitive by nature and that the profit motive is the key source of individual effort and societal advancement. Capitalism stresses individualism. In turn, this individualism accounts for the relationship of individuals to society, as follows:

> Because the good society is synonymous with the most prosperous, and can be attained only through a determined pursuit of private interests by each and every member of the society, that pursuit constitutes the individual's sole obligation to this society. Thus, because of the exclusive moral duty to serve one's own private needs and the conviction that such a course is the way to progress for all, questions of the justice of social or economic arrangements either do not arise or are deflected. The sum total of many such private decisions, and only such action, will carry the society inevitably to its next higher stage.[2]

Capitalism also stresses materialism and private property. Materialism "is the dominant (and sometimes the only) standard by which the achievements of individuals or of the economic system as a whole are to be measured."[3] The ability to own private property is an important part of this materialism. To be able to own something so as to exclude all others from using it is the central reward that keeps acquisitive, competitive human beings happy.

The community economic development movement takes an opposite position on all of these basic assumptions of the cpaitalist ideology. Taking a long-term historical view and stressing the importance group consciousness has had in the economic development of Protestants and other ethnic groups, advocates of community economic development deny that human beings are essentially acquisitive and competitive by nature, driven to success by the profit motive. Relying on studies such as McClelland's *The Achieving Society*, they note that the high achievers in society are those pushing for the attainment of community goals.[4] The supporting nature of the community environment and the cooperation needed for economic and personal achievement are emphasized. The CDC proponents also reverse the assumption of the capitalist ideology about the relationship of the individual and society. In the community economic development framework, "the achievement oriented community precedes rather than follows the physically achieving person" and it is assumed that "a relatively egalitarian ethic oriented to community benefit and cooperation are best designed to elicit achievement motivation."[5]

Because of the overall emphasis upon the physical and psychological environment of the community, the community economic development movement views the role of private property and materialism differently from the way it is viewed in the capitalist ideology. Community ownership of property is stressed. From a pragmatic viewpoint, most poor people do not have the capital to become individual owners of the basic factors of production. Hence community ownership may well be the only way left of providing material rewards to participants in the movement. Nonetheless, despite the emphasis placed on ownership, the community economic development position on materialism is quite different from that of capitalism. Material achievements are not the sole, or even the main, criteria for the success of CDCs. Services rendered, jobs created, skills developed, and nonmaterialistic values such as community pride, cultural advancement, and increasing cooperation are additional criteria for determining a CDC's success. It must be noted, however, that these are criteria for success largely because they are considered necessary prerequisites for economic success. In other words, although the nonmaterialistic criteria are valued on their own merits, a considerable amount of the stress placed upon them comes from an assumed instrumental relationship between their achievement and materialistic achievements.

This brief comparison of the capitalist ideological framework and the community economic development framework illustrates that the CDCs represent a new concept in economic development for the United States. Some might argue that the movement is basically socialistic, since many of the basic assumptions at least parallel socialist ideologies. Such as assertion would not be correct, however, even though they seek governmental assistance (a trait common to most U.S. businesses), the CDCs are not based upon governmental intervention and operation of the economy. The community economic development movement stresses cooperation and initiative by the private sector, but instead of stressing individual effort only or primarily, it stresses the role of the total community. Hence the community economic development movement is a new concept for the United States, a blend of some traditional European socialist thought and of American conservatism regarding the role of the government in the economy.

The community economic development concept is significant for poor people in that it totally rejects the famous laissez-faire capitalist doctrine of "social Darwinism" and offers in its stead a positive concrete strategy for developing and releasing the existing abilities of individuals within poor communities. The doctrine of social Darwinism "held that those who were low in economic attainments were economically unfit and therefore should be allowed to starve or die in the interest of improving the moral character and competitive quality of the population."[6] Although present-day capitalism and liberalism have moved from this doctrine to support a welfare ethic, they still stress the deficiencies of the poor economic achievers. Their nonpossession of material goods and economic skills is still viewed as the intrinsic failure of individuals. The community economic development framework makes no such assumptions about the morals, dignity, and character of the people living in low-income communities. On the contrary, the movement is prefaced on the assumption that it is precisely upon the strengths of these people in the community that economic development will be built.

A Philosphy More Compatible with Minority
Ideologies than Capitalism

The community economic development concept is also significant for the development of the disadvantaged in the United States because of the fact that the many minority groups have never appreciated the capitalistic ideological framework. Before, to be "American" meant subsuming their own philosophical assumptions about life and human nature to the dominant, white culture. Assimilation, the process of becoming similar, often meant the denial of their uniqueness and diversity.

This point can best be illustrated by citing some of the views of prominent minority leaders. Vine Deloria, Jr., in his book *We Talk, You Listen: New Tribes, New Turf*, gives the following description of the difference in the units of thought of most Indian outlooks, compared to the dominant, generally empirical, rational framework underpinning capitalism and liberalism:

> The vital difference between Indians in their individualism and the traditional individualism of Anglo-Saxon America is that the two understandings of man are built on entirely different premises. White America speaks of individualism on an economic basis. Indians speak of individualism on a social basis. While the rest of America is devoted to private property, Indians prefer to hold their lands in tribal estate, sharing the resources in common with each other. Where Americans conform to social norms of behavior and set up strata for social recognition, Indians have a free-flowing concept of social prestige that acts as a leveling device against the building of social pyramids.
>
> Thus the two kinds of individualism are diametrically opposed to each other, and it would appear impossible to reconcile one with the other.[7]

The community economic development movement appears to offer a viable means of reconciling these different conceptions. The Lummi Indian Tribal Enterprises CDC mentioned in Chapter 2 and the changes it has effected for approximately 1,600 Lummi Indians living on a small peninsula off the northern coast of the state of Washington (about a 4,700-acre reservation) provide a concrete example of the CDC's potential in the Indian environment.[8] In 1965 the annual tribal income was less than $9,000. Unemployment was sky-high, and health care was almost nonexistent. Government programs promoting private entrepreneurship and the removal of the skill deficiencies of individual tribal members were making no headway in improving the Lummis' situation. By 1973, however, the Lummis had harvested their first crop from one of the extensive and sophisticated aquaculture ventures in the United States, ten times as many Lummis were going to college, and projections were seriously being made that within a few years the average attainable net income for each tribal family would be well over $10,000 a year! The $2 million that the Office of Economic Opportunity had invested in the Lummi CDC was being transformed into 3 million fish, 30 million oysters, hundreds of thousands of silver salmon, and 50 million seed oysters—an annual output expected to gross $6 to $7 million annually before the end of the 1970s. The key factor in producing this economic reversal was the introduction of an economic development concept that was compatible with the traditional Lummi ideological framework. Entrepreneurship that could not be launched within the individualistic economic orientation of the capitalist framework could be successfully promoted within the community development framework.

The Chicanos also have a problem with the assimilation ethic. They refuse to believe that their language and values are in any way inferior to the dominant Anglo culture. They also are inclined to believe that historically they were in America before the Anglo whites. Hence they dispute the assumption that they, the Chicanos, should change.

Armando Rendon in the *Chicano Manifesto* contrasts the Chicano value system to the "gringo" one as follows:

> Our ideals, our way of looking at life, our traditions, our sense of brotherhood and human dignity, and the deep love and trust among our own are truths and principles which have prevailed in spite of the gringo, who would rather have us remade in his image and likeness: materialistic, cultureless, monolingual, and racist.[9]

> The North American culture is not worth copying: it is destructive of personal dignity; it is callous, vindictive, arrogant, militaristic, self-deceiving, and greedy; it is a gold-plated ball-pointed pen; it is James Eastland and Richard Nixon; it is Strom Thurmond and Lyndon Johnson; it is a Mustang and old-folks' homes; it is Medicare and OEO; it is an $80 billion defense budget and $75 a month welfare; it is a cultural cesspool and a social and spiritual vacuum for the Chicano. The victims of this culture are not merely the minority peoples but the dominant Anglo group as well; everything that passes for culture in the United States is symptomatic of people so swept up in the profit motive and staying ahead of the Joneses that true natural and humanistic values may be destroyed without their knowing it.[10]

The almost instinctive revulsion for the capitalist-materialist ethic that is expressed in these quotations by Rendon is probably not so explicitly felt by the average Chicano. Nonetheless, Rendon's articulation of this feeling pinpoints a major source of the Chicano problem in striving for economic success in the United States, which is that the assumptions and procedures of individualistic capitalism tend to be alien to the belief systems of these Americans. The more "brotherly," explicitly community focus of the community economic development seems more compatible with the Chicano ideology.

The concrete experience of Chicanos with the CDC organization and the community economic development approach also indicates that it might provide a reasonable alternative. The East Los Angeles Community Union, (TELACU), which was formed in 1968,[11] has brought over $40 million to the East Los Angeles area since it came into existence. An example of its activities is the Nueva Maravilla Housing Project, a well-planned 504-unit housing development that includes recreation and health care facilities and social services. Bringing together gang leaders, welfare mothers, and other residents, TELACU developed a plan for this project, which received $10 million from Los Angeles County. In order that its constituents might benefit from the jobs that would be created from the project, TELACU obtained some $.5 million in manpower training money to train residents and also secured $3.8 million in subcontracts for community businessmen.

The community economic development movement originated with black communities. Although many reasons for its development were pragmatic in nature (private black entrepreneurs and businessmen were simply not succeeding in the usual fashion), the movement also derived from a basic objection to the capitalist, materialistic stress on individualism, competitiveness, and conflict. Black Power theorists such as Stokely Carmichael and Charles Hamilton[12] stressed the need for a community organized on the basis of humanity and brotherhood rather than a community revolving around the struggle for material goods. They rejected private property as a basic value and called for the establishment of communal forms of property such as community ownership. In their view, to regain the dignity of man the sanctity of private property would have to be dissolved. They stressed the cultural distinctiveness of the black community and the cooperative heritage blacks have received from their African ancestors. From this perspective, "the goal of black self-determination and black self-identity—black power—is full participation in the decision-making processes affecting the lives of black people."[13] Further, black power could develop only within the framework of the total black community and cooperative activity within that community. It could not develop within the capitalist-materialist-individualistic framework that the dominant, white American society offers.

As in the cases of the Indians and Chicanos, the majority of blacks probably do not agree wholeheartedly with these articulate spokesmen; but again, although Carmichael and Hamilton might draw the lines more sharply than they are actually drawn in belief systems of black people in the United States, their basic point—that the dominant capitalist-materialist ethic does not prevail in black communities and that the profit motive and competitiveness are not operating to improve these communities—is valid. Whether or not the community economic development movement will actually be able to turn this situation around is a question only time can answer, but the preliminary evaluations of some black CDCs indicate that his approach may be more useful in some black communities than the more traditional approaches to economic development.

In terms of numbers of people being served and the massiveness of the poverty problem being confronted, the Bedford-Stuyvesant Restoration Corporation probably ranks first among the OEO-funded CDCs. It is also, as Chapter 1 noted, among the oldest.[14] In spite of the fact that it serves some 453,000 people in this largest black community of New York City, the Bedford-Stuyvesant CDC has left its mark just as much as TELACU and the Lummi CDC have. Between 1967 and 1973 it had invested over $33 million, much of it in housing and commercial development, both in new construction and in renovation. In addition, as Chapter 2 pointed out, this CDC has been active in outreach programs and cultural affairs and in persuading major businesses to locate offices and plants in the area. One of its most praised programs is its block renovation plan. During the summer, youths hired at $1.85 an hour are organized into teams to refurbish building exteriors. To participate, a block must get at least 50 percent of its residents to put up $50 each and sign a pledge to match improvements made on the outside with improvements on the inside. By 1973 close to 3,000 homes on 67 blocks had been refurbished, while simultaneously giving training and experience to more than 3,000 residents. Obviously this CDC has benefited its community. The 1972 finding of the OEO-funded evaluator is worth repeating: the Bedford-Stuyvesant CDC's annual job creation could eliminate official unemployment in a decade. This, of course, assumed that a major recession or other intervening factors would not interrupt progress. Clearly this assumption was violated.

A Successful Method for Economic Development

So far the significance of the community economic development concept has been said to lie essentially in the fact that it offers a workable ideological alternative to the dominant capitalist-materialist-individualist ideology of U.S. society. Because the concept more readily matches the existing belief systems of numerous minorities and poor people, it can act as an organizing and inspirational stimulus in a way that the dominant ideology does not seem to be able to do. It provides a meaningful alternative to ideological and cultural assimilation within the economic area. To the extent that the CDCs are actually able to produce economic development, they will become significant to poor people as a source of wealth, equality, and dignity.

To what extent are the CDCs successful.[15] Obviously not all CDCs are. As reported earlier, experts familiar with the CDCs nationwide have estimated that as of 1973 about two-thirds were successful. It is also true that generally successful CDCs will occasionally launch unsuccessful projects. Compared to what has happened to individual businessmen in poverty areas, however, the CDC record is excellent. For example, in 1972 in Chicago alone, 80 percent of the black-owned firms that had just been started, failed before the year was out.[16] In contrast, an independent evaluator of the OEO-funded CDCs found that 50 percent of the 250 ventures started by CDCs would be at least breaking even by their fourth year. Nationally, for small businesses in general, only about one-third live to the age of five years.

The CDCs have also attracted new loans, grants, and other investments at a leverage ratio that is comparable to what the average U.S. corporation has in attracting loans, bonds, and mortgages—$.61 to every dollar for CDCs, compared to $.65 to every dollar for corporations in general. Furthermore, according to their assessments the 30 CDCs evaluated by Abt Associates had created 2,066 permanent jobs and 5,500 temporary jobs in an average period of three years.

In addition to these hard-nosed objective indications of the success of the CDCs in the business area, there is also evidence of other successes of the CDCs in building a community sense of well-being. To illustrate, in St. Louis, Missouri, the successes of the Union Sarah Economic Development Corporation (USEDC), which serves 32,000 people in an area of 133 city blocks, have encouraged the return of private developers. One absentee landlord whose property abuts a USEDC project that is building 40 townhouses and 20 garden apartments, a parking lot, and a swimming pool has not only rehabilitated his own property but has also moved back to his old neighborhood himself.

In sum, although the CDCs and the community economic development movement are not panaceas for the poverty problem, they offer an alternative means of assisting the poor and the disadvantaged to become a part of and to benefit from the nation's social and economic mainstream. While they are not sufficient unto themselves in their efforts to end poverty, they have demonstrated that they can be foundation stones for social and economic change in some communities and supplemental and complementary institutions in others. The particular role a CDC plays, its legal structure, the problems it faces, and its likelihood of success depend essentially upon the people within the community in which it operates.

THE SIGNIFICANCE OF COMMUNITY ECONOMIC DEVELOPMENT FOR PARTICIPATORY DEMOCRACY AND COMMUNITY CONTROL

Are Community Development Corporations a New Form of Grassroots Democracy?

The phrase "grassroots democracy" can call to mind the concept that goes back to Rousseau; of direct, participatory democracy. This study has produced no evidence that the masses of the citizens within the CDCs' designated community areas are actively participating in the community economic development movement. Indeed, in many urban areas mass participation is so low, particularly in local elections, that the selection of the CDC governing board members is accomplished by appointment from community organizations instead. Hence there is no way one can validly conclude that the CDCs and the community economic development movement represent a new American form of direct democracy.

Compared to most other economic development activities and government-assisted endeavors, however, the CDCs and the movement giving rise to them do represent a type of grassroots democracy. The initial concept and the initial organizational implementations of it came from local leaders in a variety of low-income communities. No one decreed the movement from above. In fact, the idea of the movement and of the CDC organization arose simultaneously and independently in several parts of the country. From this perspective it can be said that the community economic development movement was born in the grassroots of the U.S. democratic political system.

Are the CDCs a New Form of Participatory Democracy?

From an empirical stance, in their structures and decision-making operations the CDCs are more similar to the representative forms of government existing in the United States than to any preconceived theories of direct, participatory democracy.[17] The majority of CDC members and community residents do not participate in decision making except on rare occasions; CDC governing boards have an average of 17 members. These selected leaders make the decisions and not the people themselves; and even these board members do not have complete control over the decision-making processes.

In spite of this absence of direct participatory democracy, the CDCs do operate under the assumptions of the participatory democratic framework. One basic assumption of this framework is that individuals and their institutions must be considered inseparably intertwined. Furthermore, the theory assumes that a major function of participation is educative. As Carole Pateman outlines this aspect of Rousseau's thought, the participation of citizens has in itself "a [positive] psychological effect on the participants, ensuring that there is a continuing interrelationship between the working of institutions and the psychological qualities and attitudes of individuals interacting within them."[18] More generally, Pateman states that "one might characterise the participatory model as one where maximum input (participation) is required and where output includes not just policies (decisions) but also the development of the social and political capacities of each individual, so that there is 'feedback' from output to input."[19] From this broad viewpoint the community economic development movement falls within the participatory democratic framework.

The CDCs have another similarity with this theory, in that they place great stress upon democratizing business and work activities. Pateman gives the reasons for this as follows:

If individuals are to exercise the maximum amount of control over their own lives and environment, then authority structures in these areas must be so organized that they can participate in the decision-making. A further reason for the central place of industry in the theory relates to the substantive measure of economic equality required to give the individual the independence and security necessary for (equal) participation.[20]

The community economic development movement seeks to promote these principles but as yet does not have the means to implement them in practice. The CDCs stress community ownership of property and community participation in decision making, but through duly selected representatives. Thus, while many similarities exist between the community economic development movement and the theories of participatory democracy, at this stage of their development the empirical reality of the CDCs refuses to permit considering them as modern implementations of the theory of participatory democracy advocated by such thinkers as Jean Jacques Rousseau or G. D. H. Cole.

The CDCs come closer to being a real-life representation of John Stuart Mill's version of participatory democracy. While advocating participatory democracy for reasons similar to those behind the theories of Rousseau and Cole, Mill sharply distinguished between having a voice and having an equal voice in decision making. He firmly believed in representative government, with the leaders being chosen from the best-educated and most qualified stratum of society. Mill also differed from Rousseau in that he thought that the elected representatives should only discuss and accept or reject legislation, rather than actually legislate.[21]

Community Control of Economic Development: Myth or Reality?

At first glance the relationship between citizen participation and community control would seem to be direct and obvious. Since the 1960s, however, scholars and political activists have written many pages trying to point out the differences between the two concepts. To make any meaningful and defensible conclusions about the nature and extent of "community" control over economic development in general and the CDCs in particular, it is also necessary to make such distinctions here.

According to Edgar and Jean Cahn, citizen participation has three broad values. It provides the following:

1. *A means of mobilizing unutilized resources*—a source of productivity and labor not otherwise tapped.
2. *A source of knowledge*—both corrective and creative—a means of securing feedback regarding policy and programs, and also a source of new, inventive and innovative approaches.

3. *An end in itself*—an affirmation of democracy and the elimina-
tion of alienation and withdrawal, of destructiveness, hostility,
and lack of faith in relying on the people.[22]

These values offer a succinct statement of the purposes and goals of
citizen participation: they provide a justification for citizen participation. In
this sense they are related to the theories of participatory democracy, which
also offer justifications for citizen participation.

As James Davis and Kenneth Dolbeare point out in their work, *Little
Groups of Neighbors: The Selective Service System*, reaffirmation of these
values alone provides little empirical knowledge about the actual meaning and
reality of citizen participation. "It is one thing to endorse the goals of citizen
participation and hope for their realization, but quite another to identify the
occasions and means whereby they may have a reasonable chance of realization."[23] To understand the reality of citizen participation, these two authors
declare that two separate questions must be addressed. The first question deals
with the problem of who is participating. The second deals with the issue of
how they are participating. Another separate, but related, question suggested
by these authors is, What effect does citizen participation have on the organization's capacity to do its job successfully? This study had attempted to answer
all three of these questions with regard to the CDC governing boards.

The critical point to be made about these questions, however, is that they
help delineate the difference between citizen participation and community
control. Citizen participation is the overall conceptual framework concerned
with all three of these questions. Community control is only one of at least
eight different ways a community and/or its representatives can participate in
decision making and policy implentation.

Of critical importance for this discusssion is the fact that the question
of who participates must be separated from the question of how the participation occurs and affects power relationships. As Figure 6.1 shows, there are
actually two dimensions being addressed. The question of who participates
usually concerns ascertaining whether the governing boards, regardless of how
selected, represent the general public; the specific clientele for the services
being rendered; or some preexisting elite, that is, those who usually manage
community affairs.

The second dimension is essentially concerned with the power relationships determining the direction and fate of a local institution, agency, or
program. Sherry Arnstein's eight-rung ladder of citizen participation (see Figure
6.2) helps to define the meaning of this dimension in general, and of community control in particular, relative to other possible types of citizen participation in planning and operating public programs.

The two bottom rungs of the ladders of participation are manipulation and
therapy. They designate modes of nonparticipation that are substitutes for
real participation. The next three steps are degrees of tokenism that allow

FIGURE 6.1

Two Dimensions of Participation

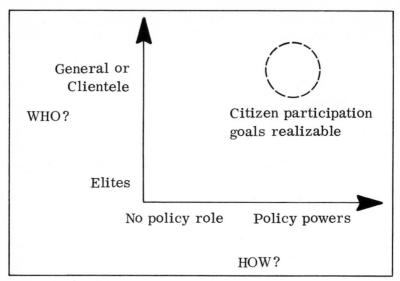

Source: James W. Davis, Jr., and Kenneth M. Dolbeare, *Little Groups of Neighbors: The Selective Service System* (Chicago: Markham, 1968), p. 227.

citizens to hear or to be heard: information, consultation, and placation. These limited forms of participation may lead to superficial satisfaction, but none give real power to insure that the participants' views will be heeded. It is only at the sixth level, partnership, that citizens can really share power with traditional powerholders. By withholding some necessary approval on some aspects of the program, the citizen-members can exercise some limited control over the actions of the traditional power holders. They can negotiate. The balance of power shifts at the seventh level, delegated power, where the delegate is directly responsible at least periodically, to the members that appoint him or her. The members can always revoke their delegation of power and appoint a new head executive. Full power through the ongoing exercise of review and control of performance is shown at the top rung, which is citizen control. At this level the poor have attained the majority of the decision-making seats and can exercise full power.[24]

Although Arnstein's definition of community control builds into it the requirement that the "have-nots" obtain control, the Davis and Dolbeare two-dimensional diagram does not. In other words, it is within the realm of possibility to have "community control" by some groups of "elites" in the latter framework, but not in the former.

This point is stressed because by nature power is a relative and relational concept. To some extent the concept of "elites" is also. In Chapter 3 we found

FIGURE 6.2

Eight Rungs on the Ladder of Citizen Participation

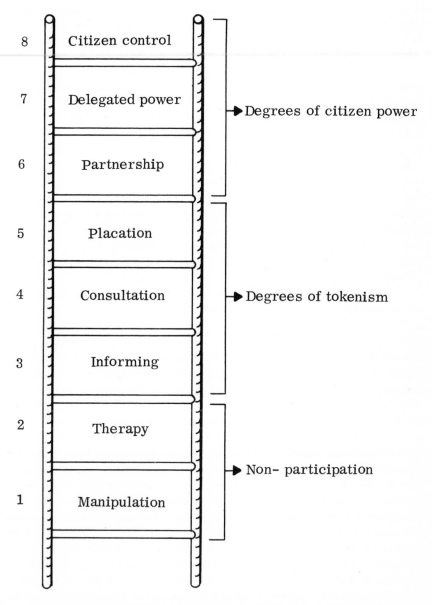

Source: Sherry R. Arnstein, "Eight Rungs on the Ladder of Citizen Participation," in *Citizen Participation: Effecting Community Change*, ed. Edgar S. Cahn and Barry A. Passett (New York: Praeger, 1971), p. 70.

that the few rather than the many participate in CDCs. We also found that the individuals who became governing board members do definitely represent a type of "elite" within their poverty neighborhoods: 79 percent of the board members sampled earned more than $6,000 a year. About 75 percent are male; 58 percent have had some college training; and 65 percent have held managerial or professional positions or owned their own businesses. Obviously such characteristics are not typical, not representative, of poverty areas.

Are these people to be considered part of the "elite" of the United States, or even of their own city- or county-wide communities? It is doubtful that they can be or in fact are. Only 11 percent of the entire sample of the 1972 governing board members earned more than $15,600 a year. Only 24 percent had advanced college degrees or even work toward such advanced degrees. About 40 percent had high school educations or less. Furthermore, in spite of the apparently high-level nature of the jobs of the governing board members, those jobs were not usually in banks, lending institutions, industry, unions, or other types of business development groups. In 1973 only about 24 percent of the 273 board members sampled indicated that they had had this type of prior work experience. Instead the data revealed that the experience the majority of the urban board members bring to their tasks as board members is wor.. with neighborhood associations (64 percent), churches (58 percent), community agencies (52 percent), and local political bodies (51 percent).

In essence the data indicate that while the CDC board members might not be exactly representative of their communities, and hence might be "elites" in this comparative sense, they certainly are not "elites" by normal standards. From a national perspective they are as representative of their communities in their socioeconomic characteristics as the nonpartisan city council members in the San Francisco Bay area are of their constituencies, where, as we noted, leadership selection is limited by social bias. In addition we know from studies on political behavior and participation in general that the very poor, the least well-educated, and the nonaffiliated tend not to participate in community life at all. Thus, until it is possible to determine more accurately what the standards for such "representative" participation would be, it seems best to conclude on an ambiguous note: the CDC governing board members can be said to be both representative and unrepresentative of the communities they represent, depending on the criteria used for assessing representativeness.

Despite this problem, the assessment of the representativeness of the governing board members in terms of their background characteristics is significant, to a large extent because of the lack of a democratically reliable means of choosing decision-making representatives from a community. The election process is less than ideal in urban poverty areas because of the extremely low turnout. Unless one is willing to assume that the fewer than 10 percent of the residents who usually turn out to vote are themselves representative of the community, elections cannot be considered reliable means of selecting leaders who are representative of and accountable to the community. The more typical pattern of the early 1970s in urban areas was a form of functional representation of the community through membership in key organizations, which in turn appointed or elected one or more of their members to be their representatives on the CDC governing boards.

This procedure obviously gives greater weight to those already active in community affairs than to those who are less active. Because the organizations that are permitted to become members of the CDCs are normally open to all residents of the same community that the CDC serves or to subsections relative to that organization, and because the selection of these organizations' officers is usually by election, the proponents of this functional-representation approach argue that the combined type of representation provides the most efficacious way of both representing the community and achieving the goals of the CDC. While this latter assertion might be true, the point must still be made that the functional-representation procedure does have the effect of reducing the amount and types of input the CDCs can get from the "common man" living in these poverty areas.

The question of how the citizens participate raises the issue of the extent of power they exercise. To what extent do the CDC governing boards really exercise community control over economic development? In her survey of community groups that had attained community control, Arnstein cited only community economic development groups as having attained that level of citizen control. Her essential criterion for reaching this conclusion was that "have-not citizens obtain the majority of the decision-making seats, or full managerial power." If one is willing to grant that having 89 percent of the governing board consist of members who earn less than $15,600 a year constitutes a majority of "have-nots," then that part of the definitional problem is met. Again, if one concedes that the governing boards adequately and reasonably represent the community, then one can conclude that the "have-nots" do have a majority of the seats.

The vital aspect of this question, however, deals with the nature of the power of the governing boards. In this study five specific functions performed by various governing boards were examined. With regard to the policy-making function, it was found that both the board members and the CDC executive directors agreed that the CDC governing boards are not the chief determiners of the policies and activities of the CDCs because OEO is. In response to questions on the types of decisions made by the governing boards, however, the board members indicated that they feel they do have a final say on CDC policy decisions and that they do make some of the most critical policy decisions for their CDCs. Among the most important decisions they felt they make are (1) establishing the overall strategy for the CDC, (2) setting goals for the year, (3) determining the kinds of businesses to invest in, and (4) making "go, no go" decisions about specific ventures, loans, and investments.

The chief limitations on the boards, according to the members themselves, come from external funding sources. The specific constraints on venture approval procedures were the ones most frequently perceived, especially by rural board members, as reducing the governing boards' ability to operate effectively. Internal restraints also reduce the powers of the CDC governing boards, but to a lesser extent than the external ones. The data indicate that the influence of the CDC board members on CDC decisions decreases as the specificity and technical nature of the problem increases. Apparently most CDC executive directors have strong managerial control over their staffs; the staffs, in turn, seem to be accountable to the executive directors, who in turn are accountable to the board.

In terms of maintaining control over the community economic development process, the two functions of supervising policy implementation and acting to prevent crises in administration are essential. It was found that 60 percent of the 172 board members queried about specific review and control functions do review the progress of the CDC in meeting milestones, schedules, and objectives. Beyond this general review, however, a majority of members are not involved in controlling the work performance of the staff. Only 48 percent of the governing board members indicated that they reviewed venture feasibility studies; 38 percent reviewed applications to funding agencies; and only slightly more than one-third reviewed the quarterly monitoring reports sent to OEO and other funding agencies.

The two specific cases that were examined to determine whether the CDC governing boards have the capability to act during crises to keep the executive director and staff under control indicated that the boards do have that ability and that specific boards have done so. The process of resolving such crises is hazardous, however; such conflicts between the director and the board can endanger, at the least, the CDC's potential success, and possibly its survival as well. The analyses suggest that the boards would be better advised to work preventively, perfecting their review and control techniques rather than awaiting for such crises to arise.

The community control concept includes the notion of public leadership and accountability of governing board members to their community. In assessing the performance of the public leadership function, the data on reporting back to the community revealed that most board members (over 80 percent) recognize the importance of their role as a link between the CDC development efforts and the community. The remaining data, however, on the more active and more politically oriented tasks connected with the public leadership function, suggest that the vast bulk of CDC board members are neither systematically nor actively involved in the performance of this function.

In sum, with regard to whether or not the CDC governing boards really do exercise community control over the economic development efforts conducted by their CDCs, one has to conclude that the boards have significant amounts of control but that the control is not full and complete. Moreover, control that is exercised tends to be exercised by a minority of board members.

THE EFFECT OF CITIZEN PARTICIPATION ON THE ORGANIZATIONAL SUCCESS OF THE COMMUNITY DEVELOPMENT CORPORATIONS

It is generally recognized that there is a necessary tension of citizen participation, particularly by the non-elites, with the type of power exercised and the organizational goals. The tension stems from the need for technical competence and expertise and the lack of it in most of the residents. The community economic development movement has received some of its sharpest criticism from persons who argue that citizen participation, community control, and economic success are totally incompatible. To address this issue, Chapter 5 analyzed the question, What effect does citizen participation have on the CDC organization's ability to do its job successfully? Judgments by OEO analysts, who were intimately familiar with the CDCs that they judged, were used to rate the CDCs studies on a 20-point Likert-type scale on success.

The findings revealed that the prior work experience of the citizens participating as CDC board members did make a difference. The CDCs of board members with prior experience in business-related areas have a higher success rating than those whose members do not have this experience, Conversely, having board members previously or currently employed in the non-profit-making and non-profit-oriented institutions of schools and universities, churches, and governmental agencies appears to handicap the CDC. Prior experience as a board member in other organizations, however, seems to enhance the CDCs' chances of success, regardless of the profit or nonprofit status of the institution or its economic or noneconomic nature.

The major focus of this analysis of the boards' impact on CDC success was the testing of 11 hypotheses about specific behaviors and tasks performed by the board members. In general terms these analyses revealed that the greater the participation of the board members in board activities, the greater the success ranking received by the CDC. However, no support was found to suggest that CDC success increased the more the board members were involved with CDC staff and its internal activities or even in all CDC decisions. Frequent efforts to use staff members' ideas and knowledge in decision making were related to higher success rankings, but more general indicators of interaction on a nontechnical level were not. It seems that interference on the part of board members in line-staff relationships is unwise, but that reliance upon the technical and professional competence of the CDC staff in decision making is wise. The data on communication processes revealed that success rankings were higher when the board members gave positive encouragement to the CDC to fulfill board-set goals and critically reviewed the staffs' efforts to attain these goals, but yet kept somewhat uninvolved in the immediate problems of the CDC staff. Conscientious performance by board members of the review and control functions was found to be related to CDC organizational success, as was the establishment by the board of specific goals, policies of operation, and guidelines. The more window-dressing types of citizen participation, such as appearing at public functions and mediating between the CDC and other local groups, were not found to be as strongly related to CDC success. It was also found that the more the board members felt motivated by community and CDC needs rather than their personal need for status and power and the greater the accountability of the board members to their target communities, the higher the success rankings of their CDCs.

These findings reveal that the tensions between the attaining of organizational goals and citizen participation do exist, but they also reveal that the tensions are not insurmountable. In contrast to what many opponents of community control would expect, the data support the view that citizen participation in the setting of goals and policies and in the supervision of policy implementation is positively related to organizational success. The lay board members representing these low-income communities abosolutely do need to defer to technical and other business expertise, but this conclusion does not also mean that community control is impossible.

CONCLUSION

Davis and Dolbeare stated at the end of *Little Groups of Neighbors: The Selective Service System* that "organizations which may be able to permit convergence of organizational and citizen participation goals are those whose missions are general in character, admitting of local variations, and which further involve public behavioral consequences inspirable through participation."[25] Community Development Corporations appear to fit these requirements. Although there are unresolved problems still needing attention, overall this study indicates that citizen participation and control over this one vital area of human activity, that is, over economic development, are not only feasible but are also positive factors contributing to the success of the CDC organizational goals. In other words, community control of economic development does seem to be a viable form of American entrepreneurship in poverty environments.

NOTES

1. The literature on capitalist ideology is abundant. In addition to Joseph Schumpeter, *Capitalism, Socialism, and Democracy* 3rd ed. (New York: Harper & Row, 1962), interested persons might profitably read Daniel P. Moynihan, *Capitalism and Democracy: Schumpeter Revisited* (New York: New York University Press, 1972); Richard Edwards, Michael Reich, and Thomas Weisskopf, ed., *The Capitalist System* (Englewood Cliffs, N.J.: Prentice-Hall, 1972); and Francis X. Sutton, Seymour E. Harris, Carl Kaysen, and James Tobin, *The American Business Creed* (Cambridge, Mass.: Harvard University Press, 1956).

2. Kenneth M. Dolbeare and Patricia Dolbeare, with Jane Hadley, *American Ideologies: The Competing Political Beliefs of the 1970s,* 2nd ed. (Chicago: Markham, Rand McNally College Publishing, 1972), p. 33.

3. Ibid., pp. 33-34.

4. For details see Chapter 2 of this book and C. M. Hampden-Turner, "The Myths and Realities of Economic Achievement; The Importance of the Community" (memorandum, Cambridge, Mass.: Center for Community Economic Development, n.d.). See also David C. McClelland, *The Achieving Society* (Princeton: Van Nostrand, 1961).

5. Ibid.

6. Dolbeare, et al., *American Ideologies,* p. 38.

7. Vine Deloria, Jr., *We Talk, You Listen: New Tribes, New Turf* (New York: Macmillan, 1970), p. 170.

8. Materials on the Lummi CDC are available on request from the Center for Community Economic Development.

9. Armando Rendon, *Chicano Manifesto* (New York: Macmillan, 1971), p. 46.

10. Ibid., p. 178.

11. Materials on TELACU are also available on request from the Center for Community Economic Development.

12. Stokely Carmichael and Charles V. Hamilton, *Black Power: The Politics of Liberation in America* (New York: Vintage Books, 1967).

13. Ibid., p. 47.

14. Materials on the CDC are also available on request from the Center for Community Economic Development.

15. Most of the major points used here to address this question come from Barry Stein, "How Successful are CDCs?" *Review of Black Political Economy* 3 (Spring 1973): 82-99. Considerable additional information is available at OEO and in the Abt evaluation reports cited earlier.

16. Stein, "How Successful are CDCs?"

17. The literature on participatory democracy has been expanding rapidly. Carole Patemen, *Paticipation and Democratic Theory* (Cambridge: Cambridge University Press, 1970), provides an excellent comparison of behaviorally oriented empirical theories of the 1950s and 1960s in the United States and those of the more "classical" theorists of democracy, John Stuart Mill and Jean Jacques Rousseau. She also presents the views of G. D. H. Cole and findings from modern empirical studies supporting participatory democratic theory. Terrence E. Cook and Patrick M. Morgan provide a comprehensive reader on this topic in *Participatory Democracy*, (New York: Canfield, Harper & Row, 1971).

18. Pateman, *Participation and Democratic Theory*, p. 22, citing Book 3, Chapter 4, of the *Social Contract* of Rousseau.

19. Pateman, *Participation and Democratic Theory*, p. 43.

20. Ibid.

21. Ibid., Chapter 2.

22. Edgar S. Cahn and Jean Camper Cahn, "Maximum Feasible Participation: A General Overview," *Citizen Participation: Effective Community Change* (New York: Praeger, 1971), p. 16.

23. James W. Davis, Jr., and Kenneth M. Dolbeare, *Little Groups of Neighbors: The Selective Service System* (Chicago: Markham, 1968), p. 240.

24. Sherry R. Arnstein, "Eight Rungs on the Ladder of Citizen Participation," in *Citizen Participation: Effecting Community Change*, Edgar S. Cahn and Barry A. Passett (New York: Praeger, 1971), pp. 72-73.

25. Davis and Dolbeare, *Little Groups of Neighbors*, p. 236.

ABT ASSOCIATES, INC. QUESTIONNAIRE

Board Members/Advisors Questionnaire

CARD 1

<u>COL</u>

1-2   SITE _____ CODE _____

3-5   CDC or VENTURE _____ CODE _____

6   VENTURE CATEGORY _____
       1 = Ventures in Development
       2 = Assisted Only
       3 = Credit Ventures
       4 = Old Ventures (IVa)
       5 = Recent Venture (IVb)
       6 = Non-Profit Ventures (IVc)
       7 = Start up Ventures (IVd)

7   INTERVIEW TYPE _____

8-10   INDIVIDUAL I-D# _____
       Site: _____
       Interviewer's Name: _____
       Date Interview Conducted: _____
       Name of Respondent: _____
       Address: _____
       Please List CDC/Venture Boards which you are a member of:

CDC/Venture name	Group	Position
_____	_____	_____
_____	_____	_____

CARD 1

<u>COL</u>

INTERVIEWER: DON'T ASK THE PERSON'S RACE
OR SEX—MARK THE CORRECT BOX BELOW.

11   Sex: 1. □ Female
                        2. □ Male
12-13   Race: 1. □ Black
                        2. □ Indian
                        3. □ White
                        4. □ Other, specify _____
            Ethnic Origin:
                        1. □ Mexican-American
                        2. □ Puerto Rican
                        3. □ Other, specify _____

14-15   1. How old were you on your last birthday? _____
            2. I would like some information on your current job:
                a. Name of Employer: _____
16   b. Type of Institution: _____
17   c. Position Title: _____
                d. Nature of Responsibilities: _____
                   (Please give a brief statement of what the person does)
18-19   e. Number of years in this job: _____
20-23   f. Current Salary: _____ per month

24   3A. What is the highest educational level you achieved?
                        1. _____ less than High School
                        2. _____ completed High School
                        3. _____ GED-received High School equivalency
                        4. _____ some college
                        5. _____ completed college
                        6. _____ some grad school
                        7. _____ Masters
                        8. _____ Phd

25   3B. What was your area of specialization/concentration?
                        1. _____ Humanities (Eng., languages . . .)
                        2. _____ Law
                        3. _____ Engineering

CARD 1

COL

        4. _____ Business

        5. _____ Social Sciences

        6. _____ Physical Science

        7. _____ Other, specify

26   4. Do you currently live in _____?

                                  (target area)

        1. _____ yes

        2. _____ no

27-28   5. How long have you been a member of the CDC or venture board?

         _____ months

      6. How often does the board meet?

         _____ times per _____

29-30   7. What percent of the meetings are you able to attend? _____

31   8. How were you selected for membership?

        a. 1. _____ open election by _____

        b. appointed as a representative of:

           2. _____ community organization serving low income residents,

           3. _____ local political group, specify _____

           4. _____ private sector, specify _____

           5. _____ business community, specify _____

           6. _____ public sector, specify _____

           7. _____ other, specify _____

      9. What particular strengths or skills do you possess which you feel resulted in your being chosen for board membership?

32   1. _____ technical skills in the areas of (the CDC's) venture development interests

33   2. _____ business experience which would assist the CDC in preparing and presenting venture proposals to sources

34   3. _____ a government background which would assist the CDC in preparing and presenting proposals to public financing sources

35   4. _____ a knowledge of the target community and the needs of its residents

36   5. _____ previous community involvement which would help the CDC develop and sustain community support for its activities

37   6. _____ previous involvement in community economic development activities

38   7. _____ other, specify _____

CARD 1

<u>COL</u>

39   10A. Do you typically perform functions in addition to attending
                board meetings which support CDC activities?
                1. _____ yes
                2. _____ no
            B. IF YES: What kind of functions?
40   1._____ provide advice to the Executive Director and/or pro-
                         fessional staff
41   2._____ perform venture feasibility studies
42   3._____ arrange for other individuals to provide assistance to
                         the CDC (specify)
43   4._____ attend meetings of other organizations as a representa-
                         tive of (the CDC), specify _____
44   5._____ assist the CDC in presenting proposals to other public
                         and private sources of funding and other support
45   6._____ other, specify _____

46   11A. Do you belong to any economic and/or local business develop-
                ment groups (e. g., Chamber of Commerce, business league,
                etc.)
                1. _____ yes
                2. _____ no
47   B. IF YES: What groups? Do you hold an positions in any of these
                groups?
48   Group   Position
                _____   _____
                _____   _____

49   12A. Are you a member of any community groups (e.g., CAP agency)
                or any social clubs or organizations?
                1. _____ yes
                2. _____ no
50   B. IF YES: What groups? Do you hold any positions in any part of
                these groups?
51   Group   Position
                _____   _____
                _____   _____

52   13A. Are you a member of any decision making bodies in the com-
                munity (e.g., School Board, Planning Commission, etc.)
                1. _____ yes
                2. _____ no

CARD 1

<u>COL</u>

53   B. IF YES: Which groups or agencies? How long have you been a member?

54-55   Group   Position

_____   _____

_____   _____

_____   _____

14. How much influence does the board have on the following CDC processes in relation to CDC staff?

	(1) Very Much Influence	(2) Some Influence	(3) Little or No Influence
56 a. _____ venture management and technical assistance procedures			
57 b. _____ goal selection and strategy design			
58 c. _____ CDC project and venture investment decisions			
59 d. _____ CDC staff hiring and promotion			
60 e. _____ Venture staff hiring and promotion			

61   15. In general, do you feel that all members participate equally in board decisions?

         1. _____ Yes

         2. _____ No

16. Do you make or participate in more decisions in this position than in other positions you have had in:

	(1) Yes	(2) No	(3) Not Applicable
62 a. stock issue			
63 b. personnel hiring and management			

CARD 1

<u>COL</u>

64	c. legal matters	_____	_____	_____
65	d. venture selection	_____	_____	_____
66	e. venture monitoring and control	_____	_____	_____
67	f. budget allocations	_____	_____	_____
68	g. generally	_____	_____	_____

69   17A. Do you feel that OEO policies or procedures place any constraints on the board's ability to operate effectively?

        1. _____ Yes

        2. _____ No

    B. IF YES: What policies or procedures:

70   1. _____ OEO/EDD venture approval procedures

        In what way? _____

        _____

71   2. _____ OEO/EDD sponsored technical assistance

        In what way? _____

        _____

72   3. _____ Policy issuances and guidelines (specify)

        In what way? _____

        _____

73   4. _____ Policies concerning board compositions

        In what way? _____

        _____

74   5. _____ Release of funds mechanisms

        In what way? _____

        _____

75   6. _____ Others?

        In what way? _____

        _____

CARD 2

<u>COL</u>

18. In general how much influence do you think the following groups or persons actually have in determining the policies and actions of the CDC/Venture?

	(1) Primary Influence	(2) Much Influence on Almost All Issues	(3) Much Influence on Some Issues	(4) Some Influence	(5) Little or No Influence	(6) Don't Know
11 a. OEO	———	———	———	———	———	———
12. b. CDC Executive Director	———	———	———	———	———	———
13. c. CDC professional staff	———	———	———	———	———	———
14. d. CDC board	———	———	———	———	———	———
15 e. CDC executive committee	———	———	———	———	———	———
16 f. venture manager	———	———	———	———	———	———
17 g. venture board	———	———	———	———	———	———
18 h. Advisory Groups	———	———	———	———	———	———
19 i. Members	———	———	———	———	———	———
20 j. Stockholders	———	———	———	———	———	———
21. k.						
22. l.						
23. m.						
24 n.						
25 o.						
26 p.						
27 q.						
28 r.						
29 s.						

CARD 2

<u>COL</u>

19. How many hours of training have you received through CDC in the following areas?

	Number of Hours	None	Not Applicable
31-32 a. stock issue	———	———	———
33-34 b. personnel hiring and management	———	———	———

CARD 2

<u>COL</u>

35-36	c. legal matters	_____	_____	_____
37-38	d. venture selection	_____	_____	_____
39-40	e. venture monitoring and control	_____	_____	_____
41-42	f. community relations	_____	_____	_____
43-44	g. other, specify _____	_____	_____	_____

NOTE TO INTERVIEWER: (This includes informal lectures to the board during regular board meetings as well as any special sessions arranged by the CDC for board member training)

20. Do you feel you need (additional) training in any of the following areas in order to make better decisions?

		Yes	No	Not Applicable
45	a. stock issue	_____	_____	_____
46	b. personnel hiring and management	_____	_____	_____
47	c. legal matters	_____	_____	_____
48	d. venture selection	_____	_____	_____
49	e. venture monitoring and control	_____	_____	_____
50	f. community relations	_____	_____	_____
51	g. other, specify _____	_____	_____	_____

52   21. Do you think stock in the CDC should be sold to community residents?

      1. _____ yes, now

      2. _____ yes, at a later date

      3. _____ no

IF YES: What purpose do you think owning stock in the CDC would serve for community residents?

53	1. _____	receipt of dividends
54	2. _____	voting rights
55	3. _____	participation in CDC activities
56	4. _____	would serve no purpose
57	5. _____	other specify _____

58   22. Do you think the CDC should distribute membership shares to
          community residents?
          1. _____ yes
          2. _____ no
          IF YES: What purpose do you think having a membership share in
              the CDC would serve for community residents?
59   1. _____ receipt of benefits
60   2. _____ voting rights
61   3. _____ participation in CDC activities
62   4. _____ would serve no purpose
63   5. _____ other, specify _____

KELLY QUESTIONNAIRE 1973

National Survey of CDC Board Members

A.   YOUR JOB AS A BOARD MEMBER:

1. Do you usually review   □ YES (if yes, do you   □ NO (if no, please
   reports to be sent to   review them before   go to question 2)
   OEO and other fund-   ____ or after ____
   ing agencies?   they are sent by the
                                Director?)

2. Do you report the Board
   activities back to community residents? (check
   as many "yes's" as are
   appropriate)
   no   □ yes, to local business groups   □
   yes, to a local CAP agency   □ yes, to interested individuals
                                      in the area   □
   yes, to area citizen association □ yes, other (specify) _____   □
   yes, to local neighborhood or
   block groups   □ _____

3. What are the most important decisions the Board has made in the
   past year? Number them in the order of importance (1, 2, and 3)
   Select three (3) please.

establishing an overall strategy for the CDC ☐
setting goals for they year ☐
determining the general kinds of business to invest in ☐
making 'go'–'no-go' decisions about specific ventures, loans and
   investments ☐
choosing the Executive Director ☐
changing the Executive Director ☐
requesting more funds and/or time from a funding source such as
   OEO ☐
investing in a MESBIC ☐
establishing or revising personnel policies and procedures ☐
other (specify) _____ ☐

4.   How many CDC related meetings have you attended in the last
      3 months? _____

5.   Do you hold a special position on the board?
      no   ☐   yes, Committee Chairman. Which? ☐
      yes, Board Chairman   ☐   yes, Committee members. Which? ☐
                                   Yes, other officer. Which?_____ ☐

B.   OBJECTIVES: How important do you think the following goals of a com-
              munity economic development program are? Number them
              in order of their importance to you (1, 2, 3). Please select
              three (3).
    Creating jobs ☐
    Developing profitable businesses ☐
    Reducing unemployment ☐
    Providing manpower training and development ☐
    Provide opportunities for local individual ownership of
      businesses and property ☐
    Provide opportunities for community controlled ownership of
      businesses and property ☐
    Reduce community deterioration (develop land, resources,
      and property) ☐
    Reduce community dependence on outsiders ☐
    Increasing incomes of those already employed ☐
    Reducing number of people leaving the area ☐
    Get outside institutions to aid in community development ☐
    Other (specify) _____ ☐

C. YOUR VIEWS ON ACCOMPLISHMENTS: On the lines to the right of each numbered item, please place a 'x' at the point which most accurately describes your views. Place only one check 'x' on each line.

1. How successful has your board been in setting goals, strategies, and policies?

2. How high are the performance goals set by the Board?

3. How successful do you think the CDC has been in achieving its goals?

4. To what extent have you received the kind of management/leadership training you desire?

D. PROFILE ON THE BOARD AND THE CDC*. On the lines to the right of each numbered item, please place a check 'x' at the point which, in your experience, describes your CDC at the present time. Place only one check 'x' on each line.

1. How free do the CDC staff members feel to talk to the Board members about their jobs?

Not very free	Slightly free	Quite free	Very free

2. How free does the Executive Director feel to talk to Board members about his job?

Not very free	Slightly free	Quite free	Very free

3. Are staff members ideas sought and used in making Board decisions?

Not very often	Some-times	Usually	Almost always

4. In trying to increase involvement and output of other Board members and of the CDC staff, do Board members stress primarily

Economic security	Status and achievement	New experiences, pride	CDC and community needs

      . . . . .
. . . . .

---

* The general form for this profile was modified from Form S in Appendix II in *The Human Organization: Its Management and Value* by Rensis Likert. Copyright 1967 by McGraw-Hill, Inc. Used by permission of McGraw-Hill Book Company and the author. No further use, reproduction or distribution of Form S is authorized.

5. Who on the Board feels the most responsibility for achieving the CDC's goals?

Mostly the director, not the board	Mostly the board chair-person	Chair-person and few others	Almost all
L_J__J__J__J__J__L	_J__J__J__J__J_	_L__J__J__J__J__	L__J__J__J__J

6. How much do you talk with CDC staff (including the Director) about achieving CDC goals?

Very little	Little	Quite a bit	A great deal
L_J__J__J__J__L	_J__J__J__J_	_L__J__J__J__J_	_J__J__J__J__J

7. How accurate is the communication from the staff to the Board?

Often wrong	Sometimes wrong	Usually accurate	Accurate
L_J__J__J__J__L	_J__J__J__J_	_L__J__J__J__J_	_J__J__J__J__J

8. How well does the Board know the problems faced by the staff?

Very little	Some	Knows quite well	Very well
L_J__J__J__J__L	_J__J__J__J_	_L__J__J__J__J_	_J__J__J__J__J

9. Who on the Board really makes the most important policy decisions?

Mostly the director, not the board	Board chair-person	Chairperson and a few other members	Almost all the board
L_J__J__J__J__L	_J__J__J__J__J_	_L__J__J__J__J_	_J__J__J__J_L__J

10. Who on the Board has the technical and professional knowledge that is generally used in decision-making (excluding consultants)?

CDC staff not the board	Board Chairperson	Chairperson and a few others	Almost all the board
L_J__J__J__J__J_	_J__J__J__J__J_	_L__J__J__J__J_	_J__J__J__J__J

11. Does the way your Board makes decisions make the Board members want to work harder to achieve CDC goals?

Not usually	Yes, a little	Yes, some	Yes, a lot
L_J__J__J__J_	_J__J__J__J_	_L__J__J__J__J_	_J__J__J__J_L__J

12. How are your CDC's goals established?

Orders by board	Orders by board and director	Orders after talks with staff	By group action of all
L_J__J__J__J_	_J__J__J__J_	_L__J__J__J__J_	_J__J__J__J__J

13. How much do staff (including the Director) resist Board-set goals and decisions?

Very great deal	Quite a bit	Some	Very little
L_J__J__J__J_	_J__J__J__J_	_L__J__J__J__J_	_J__J__J__J

14. How concentrated are the review and control functions (for evaluating employee and venture performance)?

In hands of director only	Director, board chairperson only	Director, chairperson, and a few others	Director, plus almost all of board
L_J__J__J__J_	_J__J__J__J_	_L__J__J__J__J_	_J__J__J__J_L__J

15. What does the CDC Board use cost, productivity, and other control data for?

Nothing	Policing staff	Reward and punishment	Reward Some self-guidance	Problem solving
L_J__J__J_	_J__J__J_	_L__J__J__J_	_J__J__J__J_	_L__J__J

E. BACKGROUND

1. About how long have you been a Board member?   _____(months)

2. How old are you?   _____(years)

3. What educational level have you completed?

less than high school	☐	some graduate school	☐
completed high school	☐	Masters degree	☐
some college	☐	Ph.D.	☐
completed college	☐		

IF YOU WENT TO COLLEGE, what was your area of specialization?

Humanities (e.g. English) □	Economics	□
Law □	Social Sciences	□
Engineering □	Physical Sciences	□
Business □	Other, specify _____	□

4. Your sex?   female □   male □

5. Are you: Black □   Mexican American □   White □
              Indian □   Puerto Rican □   Other □

F. PRIOR WORK EXPERIENCE: Please indicate whether or not you have had any experience working with the following institutions.

If yes, check (x) whether

	Have worked with		in managerial or professional position	as a Board member, advisor or trustee	this experience helped you as a Board member?
	YES	NO	YES	YES	YES
banking/lending institution _____	□	□	□	□	□
school/ university_____	□	□	□	□	□
local business _____	□	□	□	□	□
industry_____	□	□	□	□	□
church _____	□	□	□	□	□
business development group (Chamber of Commerce)_____	□	□	□	□	□
neighborhood association (e.g., local coop, gangs, etc.)	□	□	□	□	□
local political body (e.g., local citizen's associa-tion) _____	□	□	□	□	□
community agency (CAP, CEP, etc.)	□	□	□	□	□
Government agency (Federal, state, local) _____	□	□	□	□	□
Union _____	□	□	□	□	□

ADDITIONAL QUESTIONS ASKED OF 172 RESPONDENTS

A. Do you perform any of the following functions? if YES, indicate the number of hours per month spent on such activities.

FUNCTION　　　　　　　　　　　　　　　　　　YES　NO　HRS/MO.

　　a. provide technical advice to the Director and staff
　　b. perform and/or review results of venture feasibility
　　　　studies
　　c. arrange for other individuals or organizations to
　　　　provide business development or other assistance
　　　　to the CDC
　　d. attend meetings of other organizations as a
　　　　representative of the CDC
　　e. assist the CDC in presenting proposals for funding
　　　　and other support
　　f. review quarterly monitoring reports to be sent
　　　　to OEO
　　g. Review applications going to funding agencies
　　h. Review the progress of your CDC in meeting
　　　　milestones, schedules, and objectives
　　i. Planning overall strategy and goals for the CDC
　　　　5, 10, 15 years from now
　　j. Other (Specify) _____

B. Do you report Board activities back to community residents?
　　_____yes; _____no
　　IF YES, PLEASE COMPLETE THE FOLLOWING:

Do you report to:	Yes	No	If YES, is the report Written	Oral	No. of Reports a month
A local CAP agency					
Area citizen associations					
Local neighborhood or block groups					
Local business groups					
Interested individuals in the area					
Other (Specify) _____					

2. What type of information do you report? (Check as many as you need).
_____ (a) New areas of investment
_____ (b) progress toward specific goals
_____ (c) financial status of the CDC
_____ (d) problems with the Board and the CDC staff
_____ (e) differences of opinion between Director and Board
_____ (f) plans and strategies for the future
_____ (g) CDC action taken on loans and ventures
_____ (h) benefits they can expect to get from the CDC's operation
(Specify) _____
_____ (i) Other. Specify _____

C. Please number the following items according to how important such training would be for you; that is, which would you want to take first, second, third. Please select three (3) at least*

ORDER OF
IMPORTANCE   TRAINING ON

_____ What community economic development is all about?
_____ Board responsibility to funding source (for example, to OEO)
_____ Board responsibility to community
_____ Corporate management (esp. personnel policies)
_____ Relationships of Board to Executive Director (duties differences in jobs)
_____ Reading financial reports
_____ Nature of OEO, OMBE, and their effect on CDCs
_____ Significance of the National Congress of Community Economic Development
_____ How to report back to community
_____ Role of Board in planning and setting CDC goals about what CDC and the community should achieve in 5, 10, or 15 years from now
_____ Use of procedural rules in meetings (parlimentary procedure)
_____ How to work with problem staff and/or problem Board members
_____ Others (please specify)

---

*The data from this question are reported in a separate publication, CDC CDC Board Training Needs: The Result of Two Surveys (Cambridge, Mass.: Center for Community Economic Development, 1974).

KELLY 1973 QUESTIONNAIRE FOR OEO PERSONNEL

NAME OF THE CDC _____

1. How successful has this Board been in setting goals, strategies, and policies?

2. Has this CDC significantly affected community economic development in its area?

3. Compared to all other CDCs, how difficult is the economic environment of this area?

4. Compared to all other CDCs, how difficult is the political environment of this area?

5. How successful do you think this CDC has been in achieving its goals?

6. Indicate which goals you have used in evaluating this CDC's success. Rate them 1, 2, 3 in their order of importance.
   _____ Creating jobs
   _____ Developing profitable businesses
   _____ Reducing unemployment
   _____ Providing manpower training and development
   _____ Provide opportunities for local individual ownership of businesses and property
   _____ Provide opportunities for community controlled ownership of businesses and property
   _____ Reduce community deterioration (develop land, resources & property)
   _____ Reduce community dependence on outsiders
   _____ Increasing incomes of those already employed
   _____ Reducing number of people leaving the area
   _____ Get outside institutions to aid in community development
   _____ Other (please specify)

7. Do you think this CDC would be more successful if it followed different goals?   _____ Yes;   _____ No
IF YES: Please indicate by the letters a, b, & c, in item 6 what these different goals would be.

ABOUT THE AUTHOR

RITA MAE KELLY is an associate professor in the Department of Urban Studies and Community Development at Rutgers, The State University of New Jersey, Camden, New Jersey. From 1973 to 1975 she was director of a national survey of the leadership of community development corporations for the Center for Community Economic Development, Cambridge, Massachusetts. Holder of a Ph.D in Political Science from Indiana University (1967), she has also been a lecturer in political science for the University of Maryland Overseas Division (1965-67) and Seton Hall University (1974-75), a Research Scientist at American University (1968-69), a Senior Research Scientist for American Institutes for Research (1969-72), a consultant to the Office of Economic Opportunity (1972-73), and a consultant to various private and public research groups.

Her publications include *The Pilot Police Project: A Description and Assessment of a Police-Community Relations Experiment in Washington, D.C.* and *The Making of Political Women: A Study of Socialization and Role Conflict*. Dr. Kelly has also written a variety of articles, book chapters, and monographs on the leadership of Community Development Corporations, on public policy, on the study of ideology, on the Soviet Union, on social change, on police-community relations, on race relations, on the development of political women, and on evaluation research. Her articles have been published in such journals as *The Journal of Social Issues*, the *Journal of Applied Psychology*, the *Journal of Comparative Political Studies*, the *Journal of Comparative and International Public Policy*, *Soviet Studies*, *Marab*, and *Sex Roles*.

Her papers on these and related methodological topics have also been delivered at meetings of the American Political Science Association, American Psychological Association, the International Studies Association, the Southern Political Science Association, New Jersey Political Science Association, and District of Columbia Sociological Society, as well as to national conferences of various churches and economic development groups.

FEDERAL GRANTS-IN-AID: Maximizing Benefits to the States
Anita S. Harbert

MINORITY ACCESS TO FEDERAL GRANTS-IN-AID: The Gap Between Policy and Performance
John Hope, II

PATTERNS OF DECISION MAKING IN STATE LEGISLATURES
Eric M. Uslaner
Ronald E. Weber

POLICY EVALUATION FOR COMMUNITY DEVELOPMENT: Decision Tools for Local Government
Shimon Awerbuch
William A. Wallace

THE SOCIAL IMPACT OF REVENUE SHARING: Planning, Participation, and the Purchase of Service
Paul Terrell
with the assistance of
Stan Weisner

WELFARE POLICY MAKING AND CITY POLITICS
Sharon Perlman Krefetz